A course for ADULT beginners

ALAN **HAUGHTON** and
CHRIS **TAMBLING'S**
Play Piano!
BOOK 1

kevin
mayhew

kevin mayhew

First published in Great Britain in 2007 by Kevin Mayhew Ltd
Buxhall, Stowmarket, Suffolk IP14 3BW
Tel: +44 (0) 1449 737978 Fax: +44 (0) 1449 737834
E-mail: info@kevinmayhewltd.com

www.kevinmayhew.com

© Copyright 2007 Kevin Mayhew Ltd.

The music in this book is protected by copyright and may not be reproduced
in any way for sale or private use without the consent of the copyright owner.

9 8 7 6 5 4 3 2 1

ISBN 978 1 84417 784 4
ISMN M 57024 770 7
Catalogue No. 3612167

Designer: Sara-Jane Came
Layout and Typesetting: Chris Coe
Music Setter: Donald Thomson
Proof-reader: Sarah Stirling

Printed and bound in Great Britain

A note for you . . .

Play Piano! takes you on a journey from your very first steps on the piano to about Grade 1 level in two books. Straightforward and progressive, the **Play Piano!** books for adult beginners contain a wealth of both popular and new music to learn and play.

Whether you are new to the piano or revisiting the instrument after a break, these books provide everything you need. Enjoy!

Alan Haughton

for your teacher . . .

Coverage of **Play Piano!**, Book 1

- Staves – treble clef: middle C – C
- bass clef: C – middle C
- Notes and rests: crotchet, minim, dotted crotchet, dotted minim, semibreve, quaver
- $\frac{4}{4}$ and $\frac{3}{4}$ and $\frac{2}{4}$
- Fingers and fingering
- Posture
- Bars and bar lines
- *p* – piano, *f* – forte, *pp* – pianissimo, *ff* – fortissimo,
- *mp* – mezzo piano, *mf* – mezzo forte
- Legato and staccato
- Intervals – 2nd and 3rd
- Finger workouts
- ⟨———⟩ ⟨———⟩ (crescendo or cresc. and diminuendo or dim.)
- Chords
- Repeat signs
- Patterns in music
- Scale – C major
- Italian Words – adagio, andante, moderato, allegretto, allegro
- Quiz pages for revision and reinforcement
- *D.C. al Fine*

Contents

On the CD, the pieces have two bars of clicks as an introduction. Throughout the book CD Tracks are shown by

	Page	CD Track
Rhythm Workout 1	6	1
Grandfather Clock	6	2
The Tortoise . . .	8	3
. . . and the Hare	8	4
Fish and Chips	9, 10	5
Cold Water	9, 10	6
Let's Go!	9, 10	7
Walk the Dog	11	8
Red Peppers	11	9
Beach Party	11	10
Lazy Day	12	11
Boogie Roll	12	12
Entry of the Gladiator	12	13
Morning	13	14
Rock Solid	13	15
Left-hand Workouts	14	16
Off to Town	14	17
Jump to It	14	18
Rhythm Workout 2	15	19–22
Three's Company	15	23
The Beach	16	24
Jamaica Hello	16	25
Musette	17	26
German Folk Tune	17	27
Right-hand Workouts	18	28
Left-hand Workouts	18	29
Pogo Waltz	19	30
March Past	20	31
Left-hand Workouts	22	32
Fanfare	22	33
When the Saints Go Marching In	23	34
Merrily We Roll Along	24	35
Go for Gold	25	36
Swing It	25	37
Rhythm Workout 3	26	38–40
Finger Workout	26	41–42
Clog Dance	27	43
Hard Rock	28	44
Copycat	29	45
Country Dance	29	46
Dawn	30	47
Dynamic Study	31	–
Uptown	31	48

	Page	CD Track
Hop It!	33	49
Highway	33	50
The Banks of the Ohio	34	51
Ode to Joy	35	52
Jogging	36	53
Take a Break	36	54
Bouncing Bean	37	55
Razzle Dazzle	37	56
Step on It	38	57
Hot Cross Buns	39	58
Bass Dance	39	59
Fiddlesticks	39	60
Super Trouper	40	61
French Folk Song	41	62
Rhythm Workout 4	42	63–67
Hop, Skip and Jump	42	68
Pineapple	43	69
1, 2, 3, Go!	43	70
The Rock	45	71
The Sprial Staircase	45	72
Gopak	46	73
Pick up Sticks	47	74
After the Storm	48	75
Cockles and Mussels	49	76
Shepherd's Hey	50	77
Roxy's Waltz	51	78
Rhythm Workout 5	52	79–81
Jog It!	52	82
1, 2, 3	53	83
Slalom	53	84
Walk Tall	54	85
High Street Rag	55	86
Rhythm Workout 6	56	87–89
Donkey Riding	56	90
Snail	57	91
Cycling	57	92
Thumb Workout	59	93
On the Scales	59	94
Jump to It	60	95
Butterfingers	60	96
Popeye the Sailor Man	62	97
Papillion (Butterfly)	63	98
Jingle Bells	64	99

The Piano Keyboard

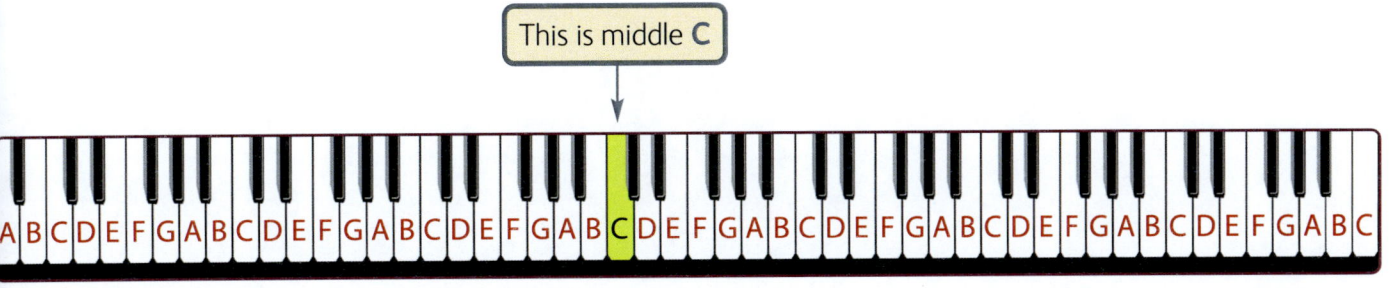

Low notes · High notes

Know This

Music is written on lines and spaces called the **stave**.

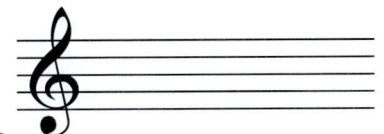

This is a **treble clef**

– the music for the right hand is usually written on the treble stave.

The **time signature** tells us there are four beats in a bar, like this:

These are one-beat notes called **crotchets** (or quarter-notes).

Rhythm Workout 1

Most music has a pulse – a regular, underlying beat.
A ticking clock has a regular, even pulse. We can write this pulse as a rhythm like this:

1

Tick tock tick tock   tick tock tick tock   tick tock tick tock   tick tock tick tock

Tap these notes. Keep in time with the CD and try to keep the beats even and regular.

We can sort the line of notes into four-beat groups using **bar lines**.

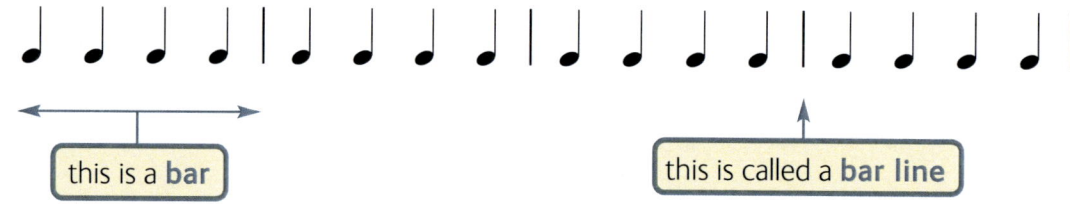

this is a **bar**   this is called a **bar line**

Grandfather Clock

Tap this rhythm twice through in time with the tune on the CD.
There is a two-bar music introduction.

2

Let's Get Started . . .

> **Know This**
>
> The fingers are numbered 1–5 on both hands.
>
>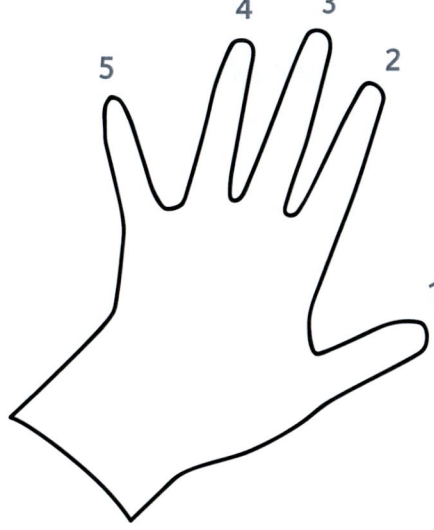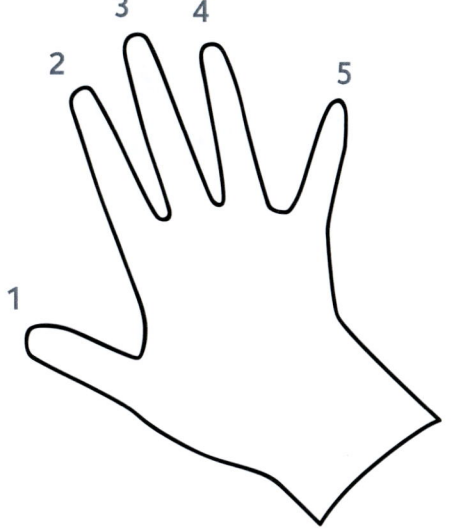

> **Top Tip**
>
> Sit at a height where your arms are parallel to the keyboard.

Middle C

Note

Middle C is written on its own line under the treble stave.

Middle C is in the middle of the piano keyboard

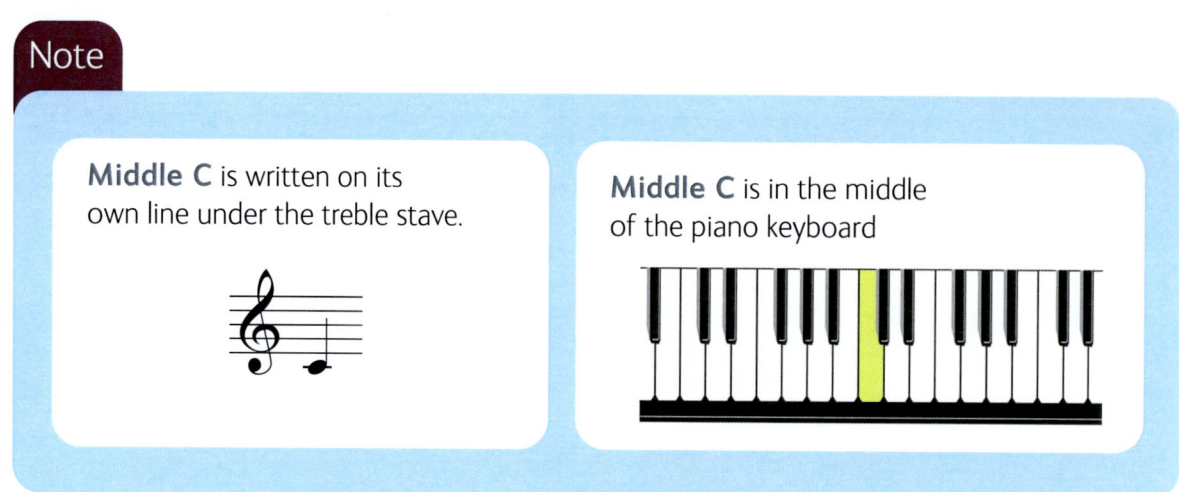

Play these tunes using the right-hand thumb. Notice the different speeds.

The Tortoise . . .

Slowly — Play twice

. . . and The Hare

Quickly — Play twice

Top Tip

Try to keep your fingers slightly curved – as though you are holding a small ball.

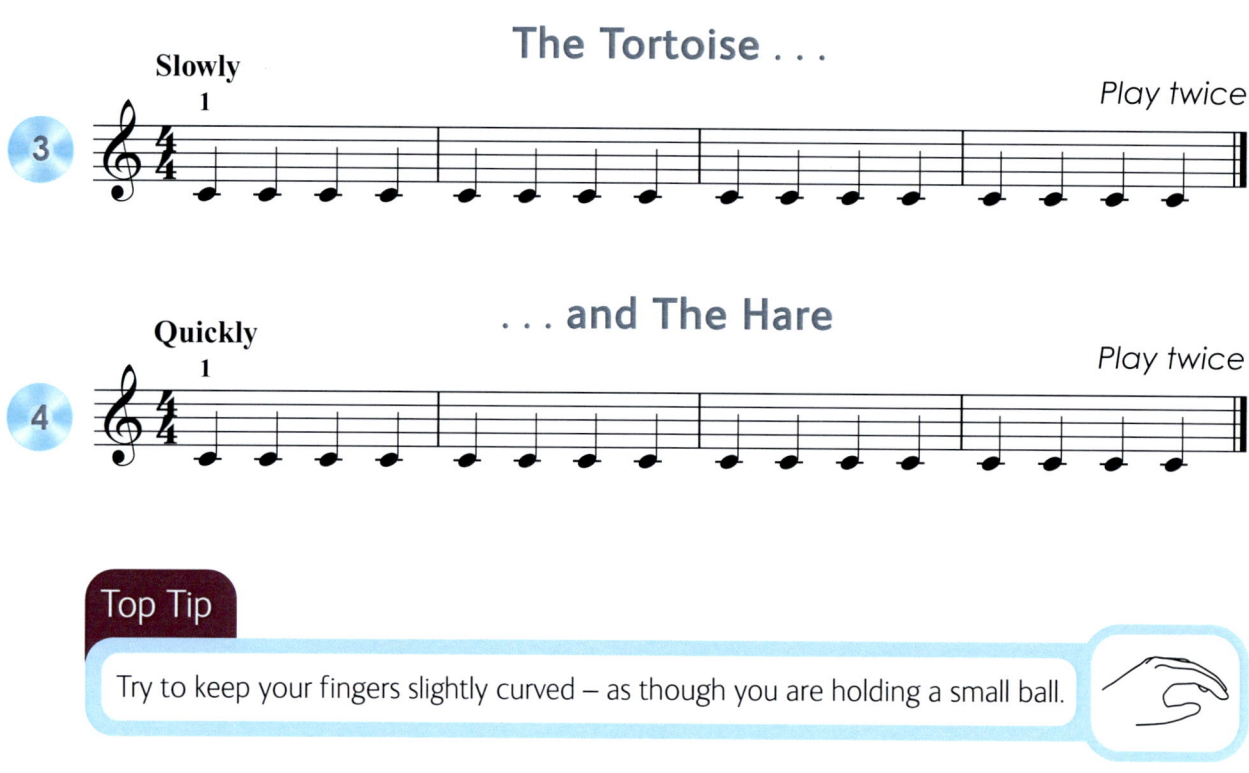

The Tortoise . . .

. . . and The Hare

Crotchet Rest

Know This

One-beat (crotchet) **rest** – you don't play for one beat

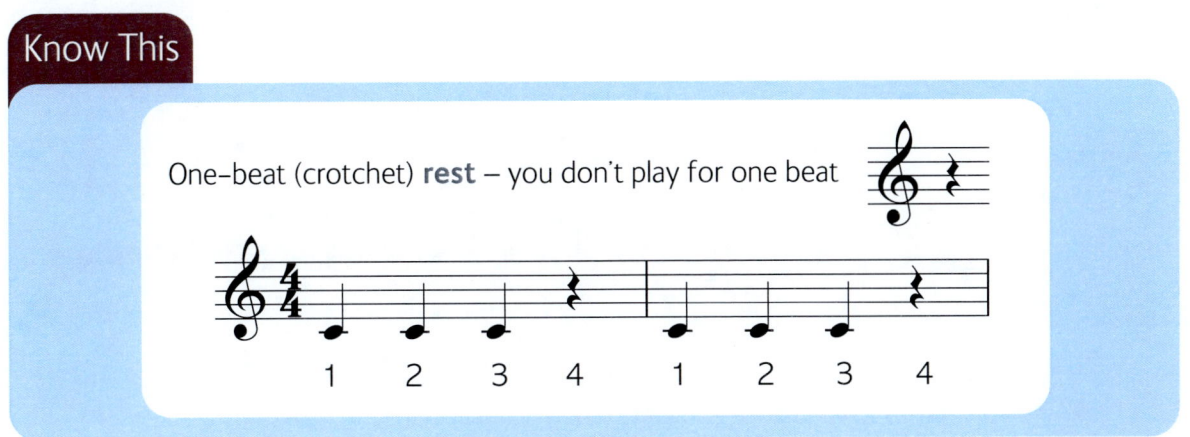

Now try playing the tunes you have learnt using different C's on the piano.

Left-hand C

Note

This is the **bass clef**. The music for the left hand is usually written here.

This is **left-hand C**, the one to the left of **Middle C**.

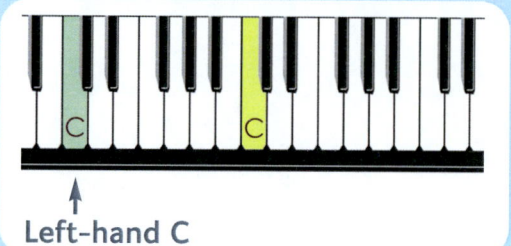

Try these. Use the left-hand 5th finger on left-hand C.

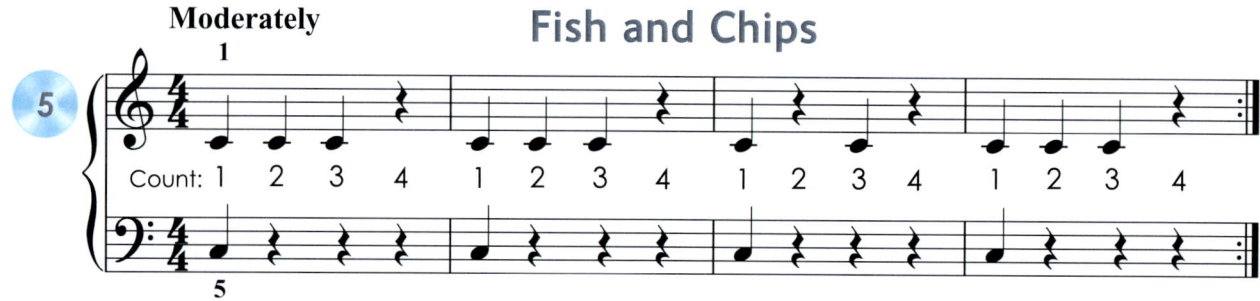

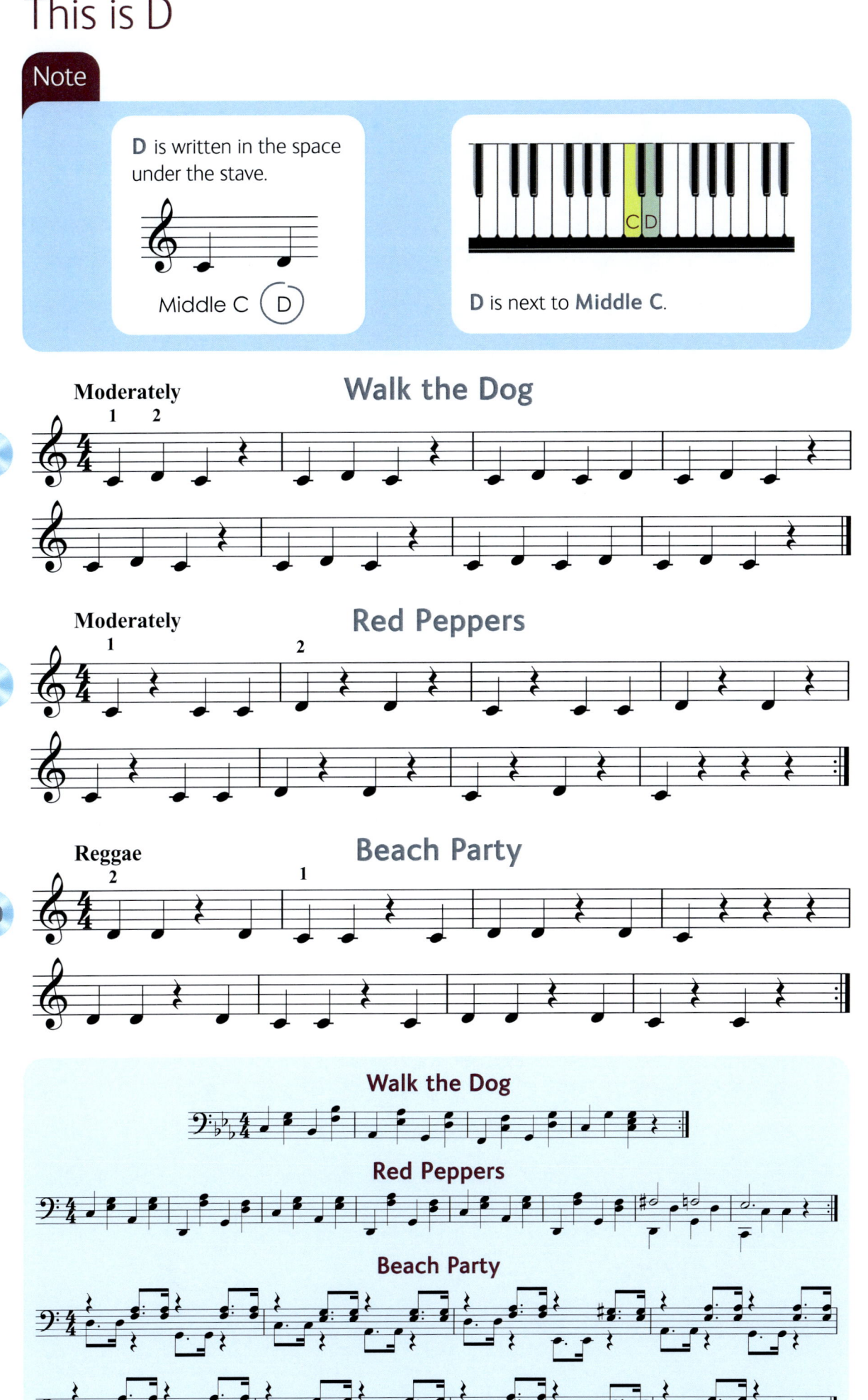

Minims

Know This

These are two-beat notes called **minims** (or half-notes).

The **minim rest** sits on the middle line.

This is E

Note

E is written on the bottom line of the treble stave.

E is next to D.

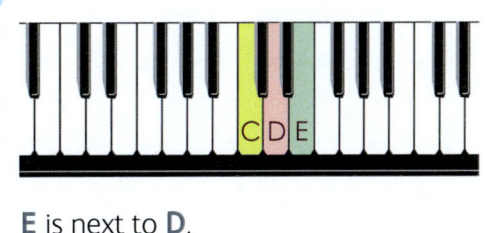

Morning

Know This

p (piano) = play quietly ***f*** (forte) = play loudly

Dynamics is a word used in music to describe how loudly or quietly notes should be played

Top Tip

Look out for the repeat signs!

Rock Solid

Morning

Rock Solid

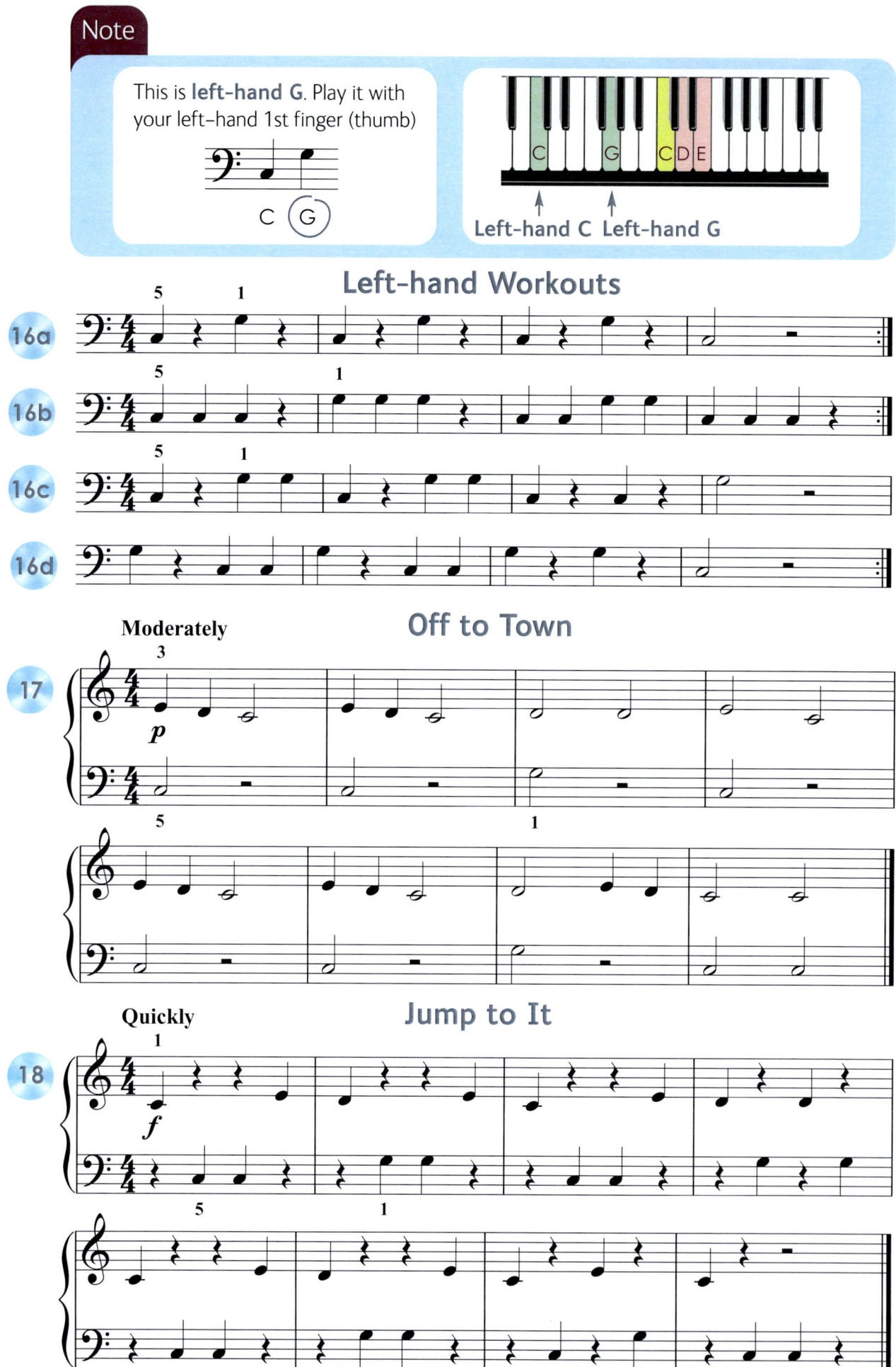

3/4 Time

Know This

The 3 in the time signature tells us there are three beats in a bar. The dot by the minim turns it into a three-beat note called a **dotted minim**. The dot by the minim rest turns it into a three-beat rest.

Tap, then play these tunes.

Rhythm Workout 2

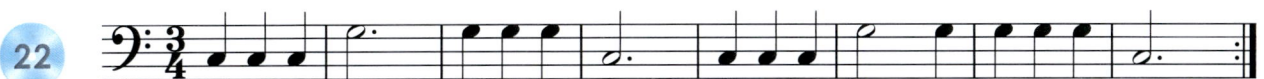

Three's Company

15

This is F

Note

F is written on the first space of the treble stave.

Middle C   D   E   (F)

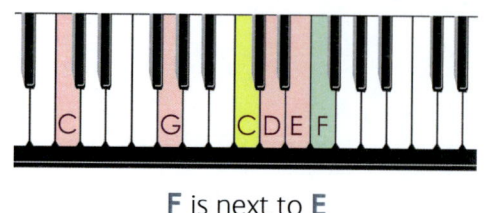

F is next to **E**

Top Tip

Practise these tunes hands separately first.

The Beach

Moderately

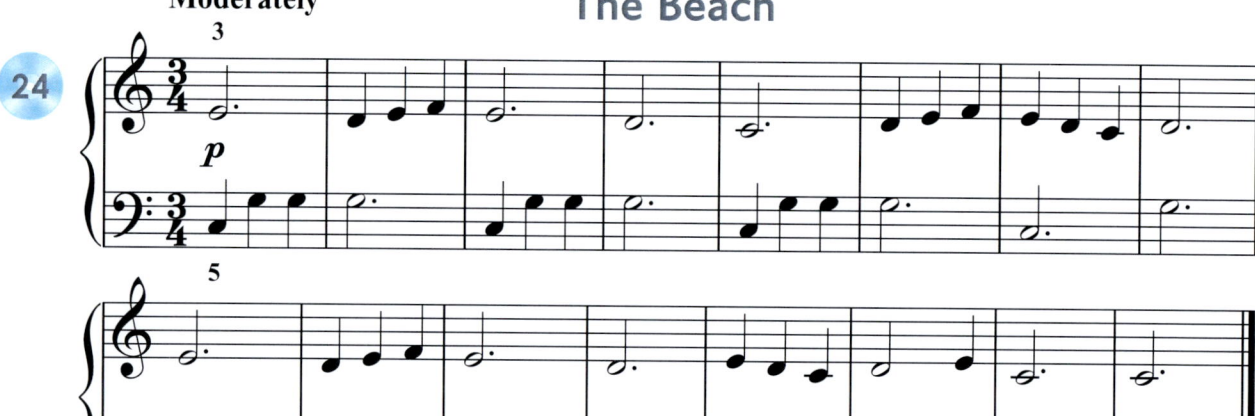

24

Know This

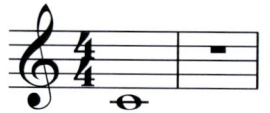

This is a four-beat note. It is called a **semibreve** or whole note.

The semibreve rest hangs from the 4th line. It is also used to show a whole bar's rest, whatever the time signature.

Jamaica Hello

Calypso

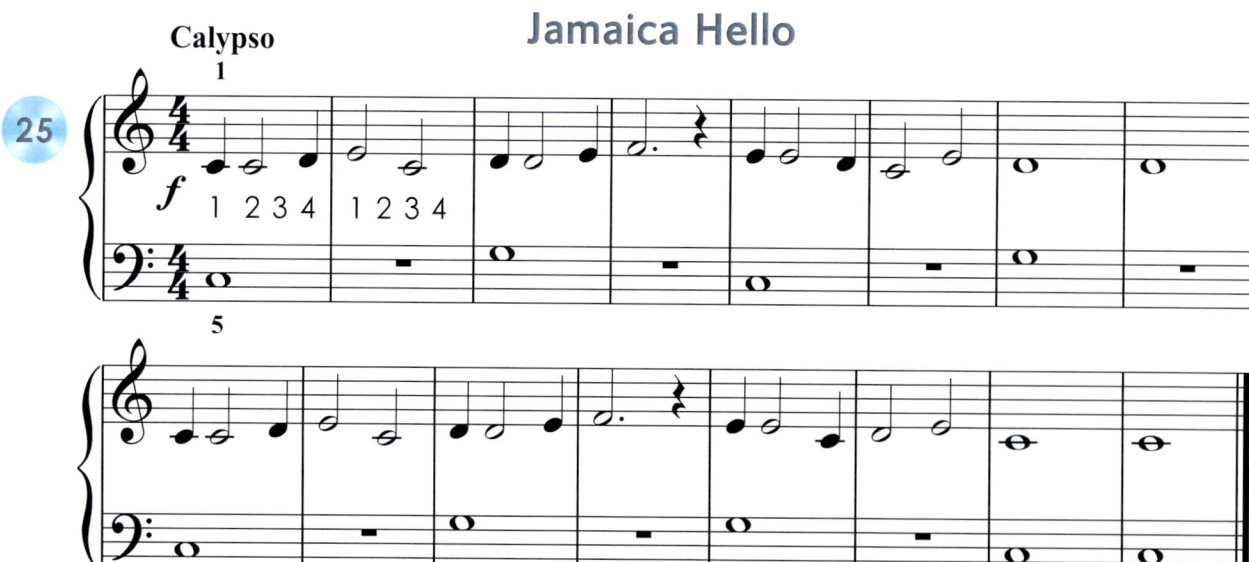

25

16

At the Gym

Try these finger workouts.

Right-hand Workouts

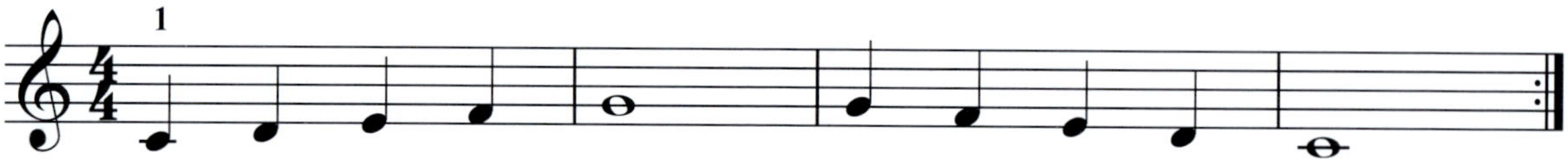

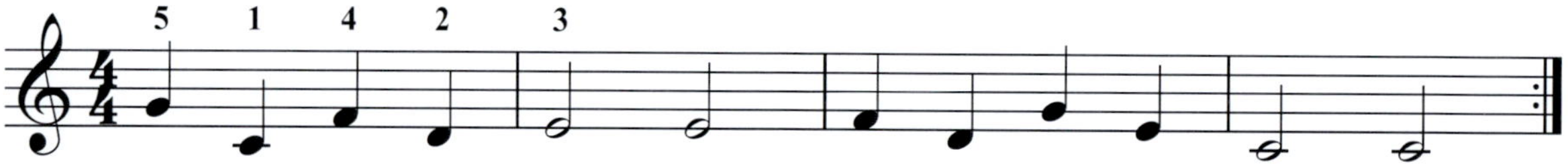

Know This

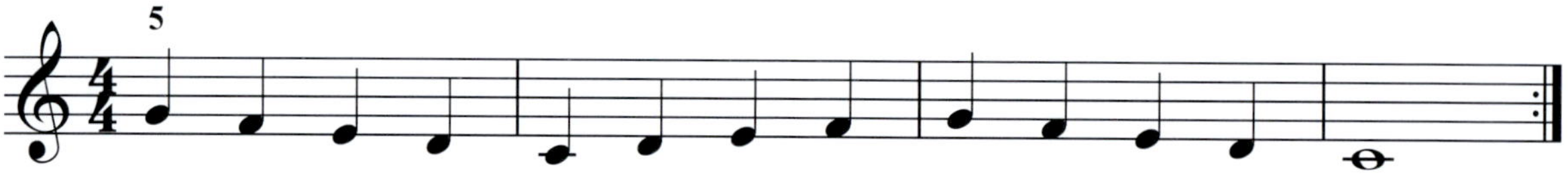

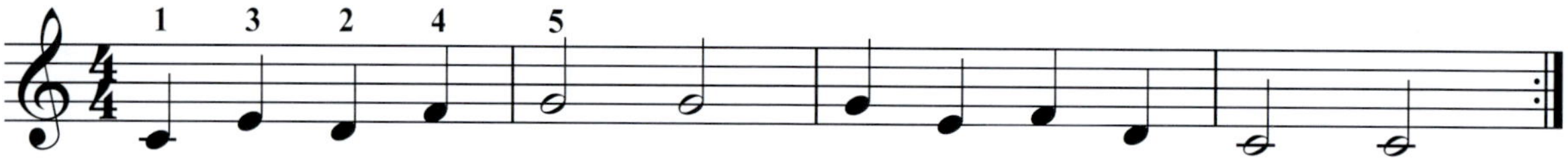

A chord is made when you play two or more notes at the same time. These are chords:

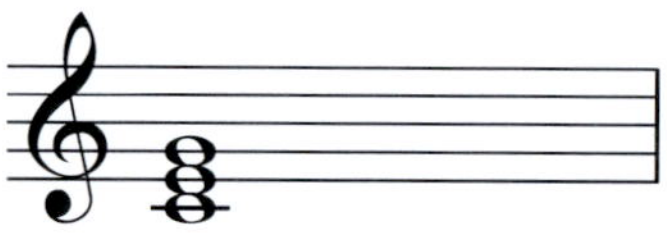

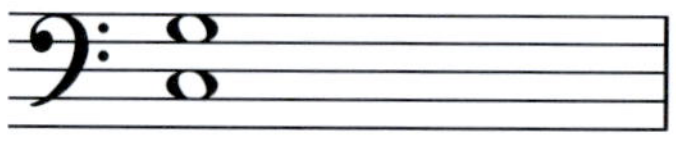

Make up some chords of your own – sweetly harmonious or devilishly dissonant?

Left-hand Workouts

Congratulations!

Note

You now know these notes:

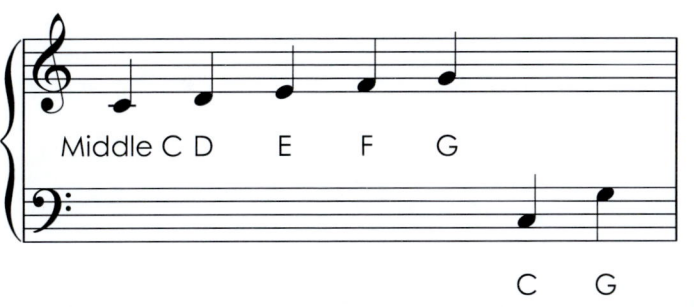

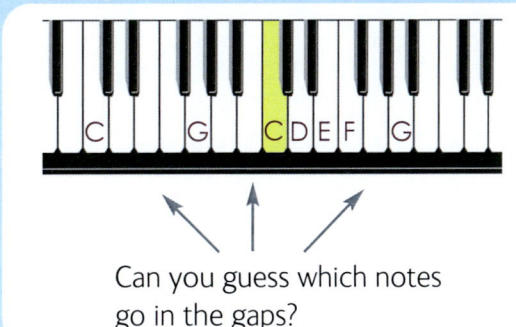

Can you guess which notes go in the gaps?

Know This

More dynamics:

pp (pianissimo) = play very quietly

ff (fortissimo) = play very loudly

Pogo Waltz

March Past

Quiz Time

How many beats? **What is the note's name?**

♩ _____ _____

𝅗𝅥 _____ _____

𝅗𝅥. _____ _____

𝅗𝅥 _____ _____

How many beats are these rests worth?

_____   _____

What do these letters mean?

f   *p*

_____   _____

Can you name these notes?

How many beats in a bar?

_____   _____

What do these signs mean?

_____

What is a chord?

_____

_____

Filling the Gaps

The notes **D**, **E** and **F** come between **C** and **G**.

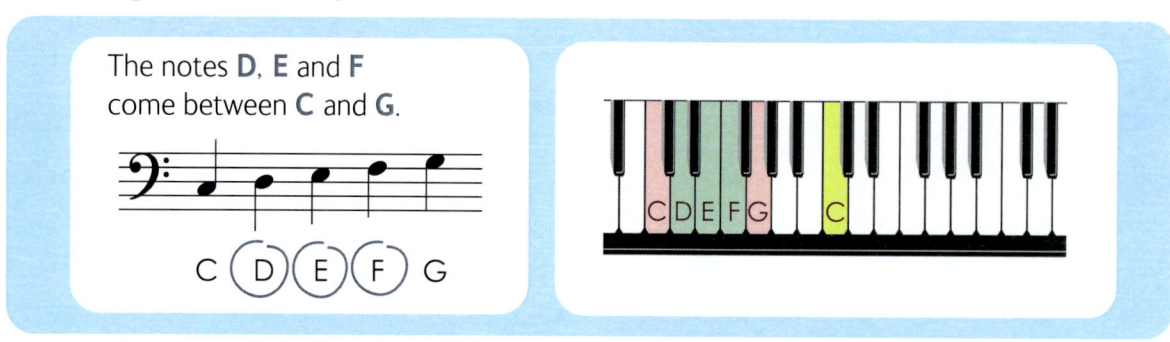

Left-hand Workouts

32a

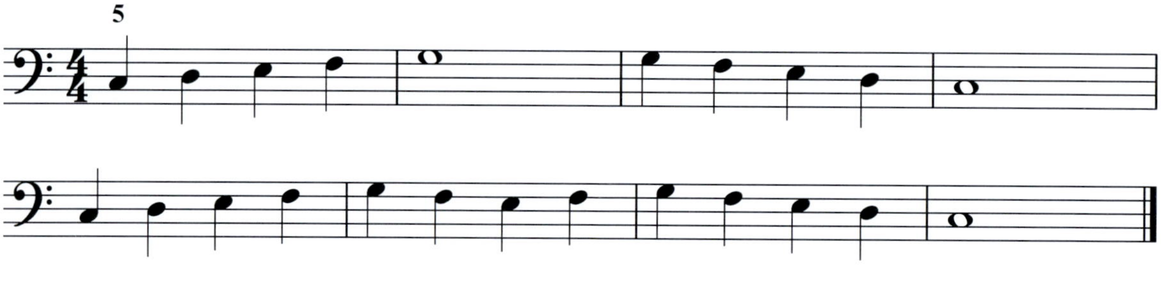

32b

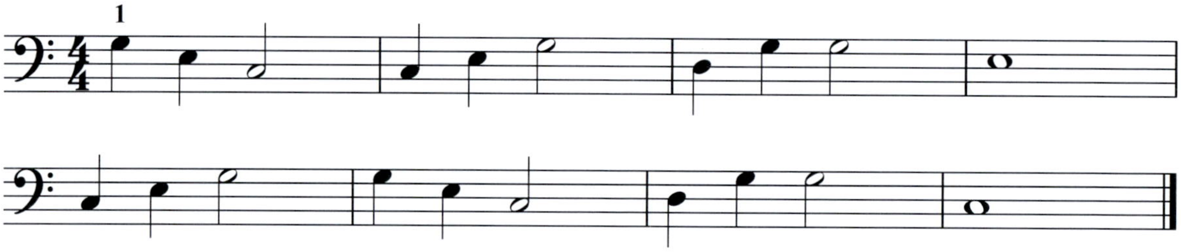

32c

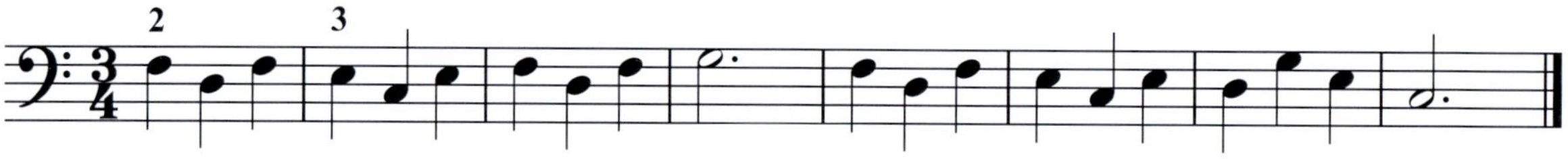

Fanfare

33

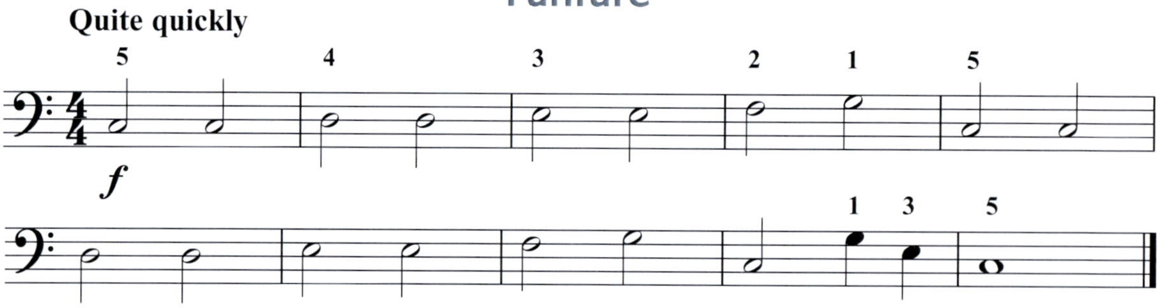

Fanfare

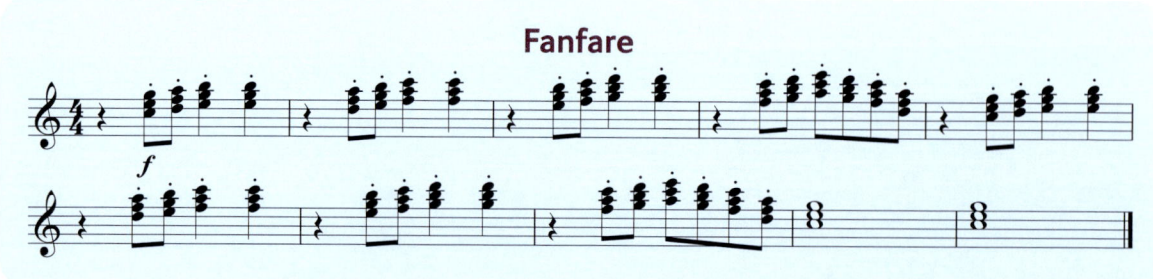

When the Saints Go Marching In

Trad. arr. Alan Haughton

Merrily We Roll Along

Trad. arr. Alan Haughton

(Bring out the tune in the left hand)

Tails Up or Down?

Know This
- Notes below the middle line have tails up.
- Notes above the middle line have tails down.
- Notes on the middle line can have tails up or down.

Go for Gold
36 Moderately

Swing It
37 Slowly

Add tails to these notes:

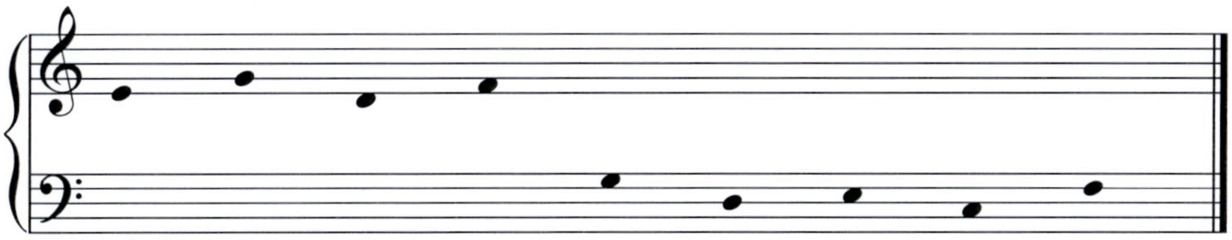

Go for Gold

Swing It

25

Quavers

Know This

Quavers are half-beat notes. (They are also called eighth-notes.) Together, two quavers take up the same time as one crotchet.

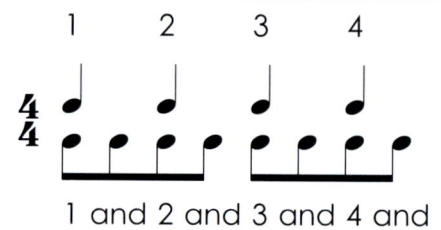

Know This

Quavers can be grouped in twos or fours.

Rhythm Workout 3

Tap these rhythms.

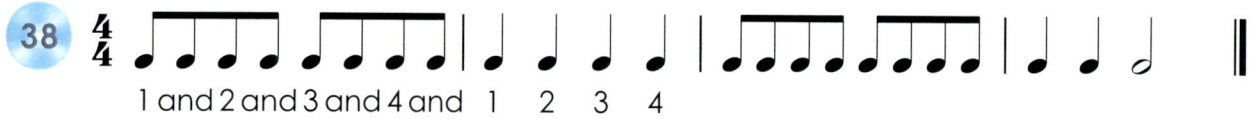

Finger Workouts

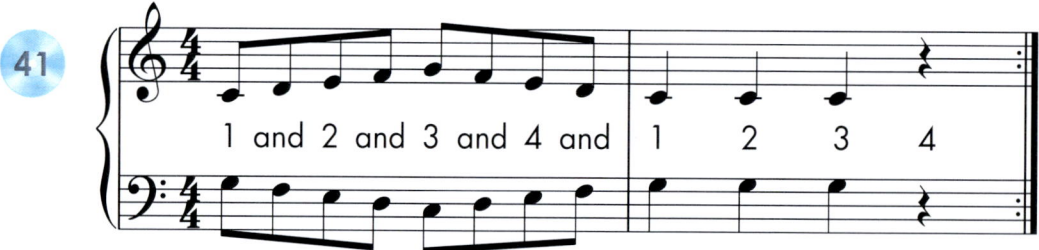

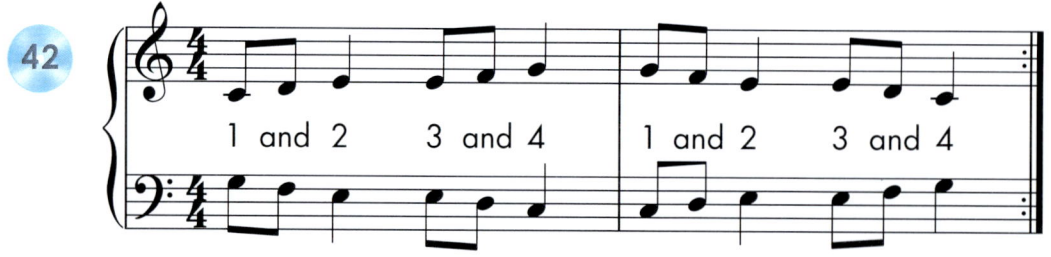

Clog Dance

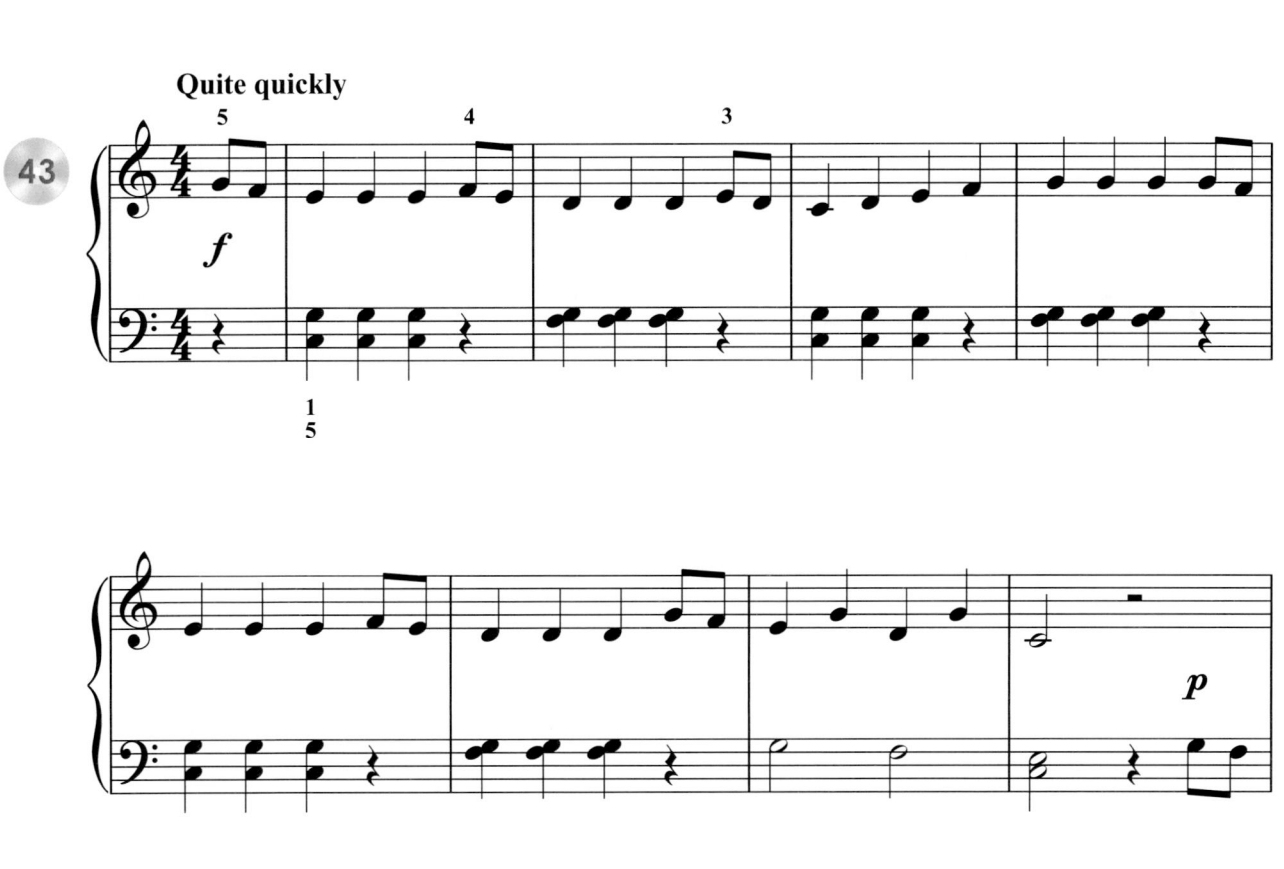
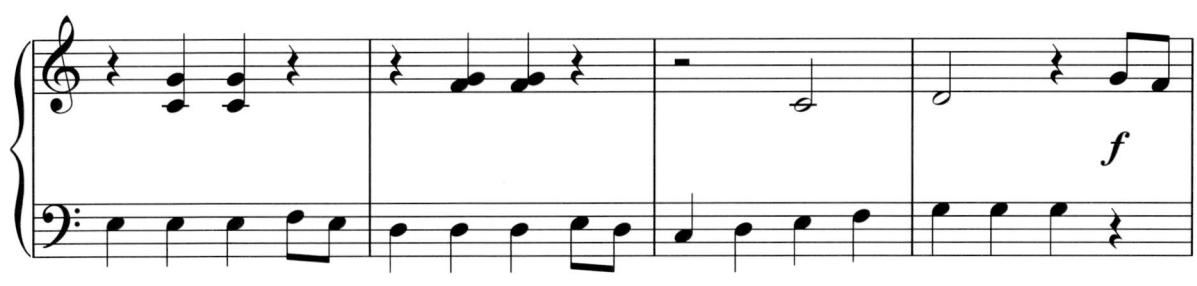

Hard Rock

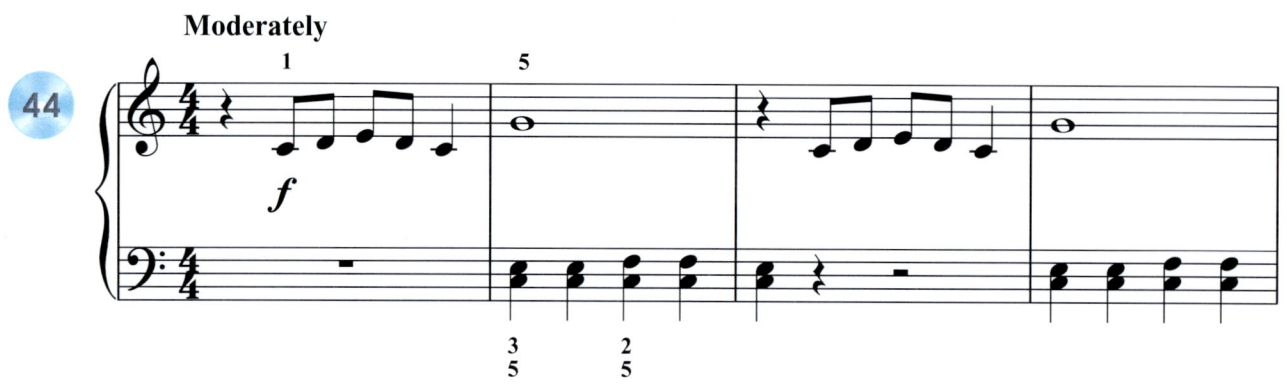

Patterns

Music is made up of patterns of rhythm and melody.

Before you learn these pieces, can you find any patterns of rhythm or melody? Are any patterns repeated?

Copycat

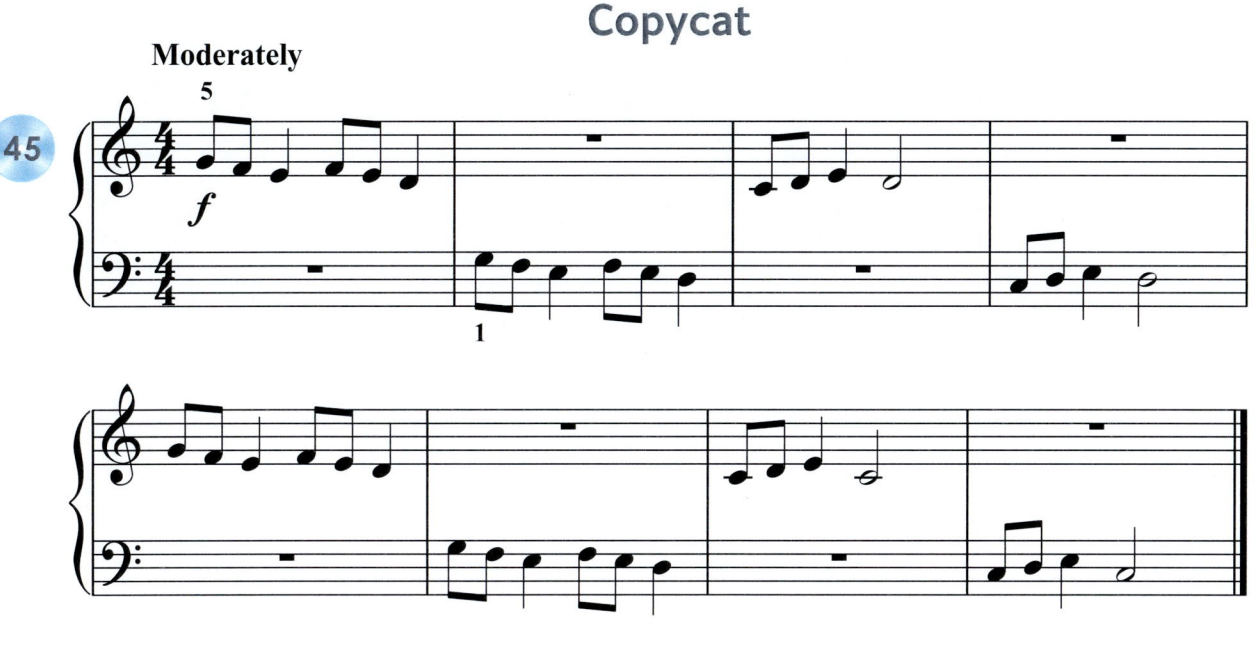

Country Dance

mp and *mf*

Know This

More dynamics:

mp (mezzo piano) = play moderately quietly

mf (mezzo forte) = play moderately loudly

Dawn

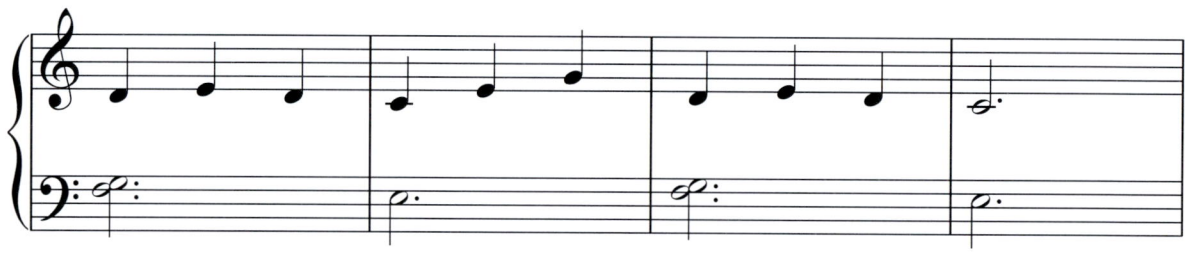

Crescendo and Diminuendo

Know This

Even more dynamics:

```
━━━━◁  = crescendo or cresc. (get gradually louder)

▷━━━━  = diminuendo or dim. (get gradually quieter)
```

Dynamic Study

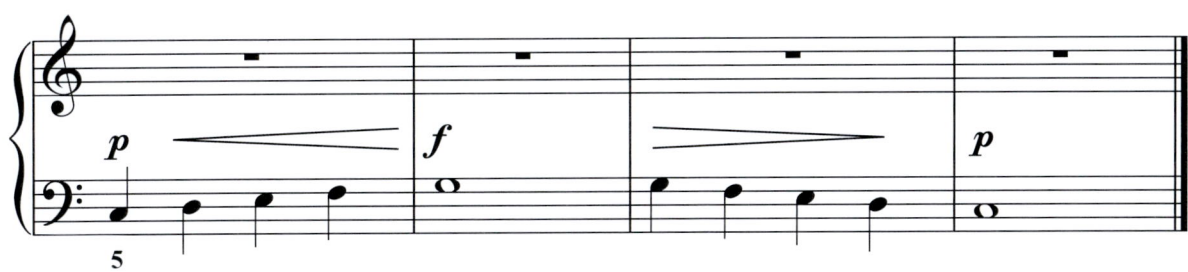

Uptown

Intervals

An interval is the distance from one note to another.

Know This

A 2nd –
is from one line to the next space (up or down)
or from one space to the next line (up or down).

Know This

A 3rd –
is from one line to the next line (up or down)
or from one space to the next space (up or down).

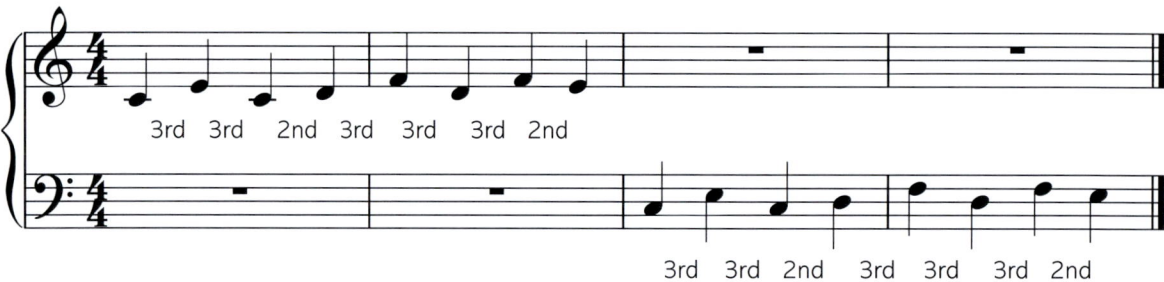

2nd or 3rd?

Write in the answers.

Hop It!

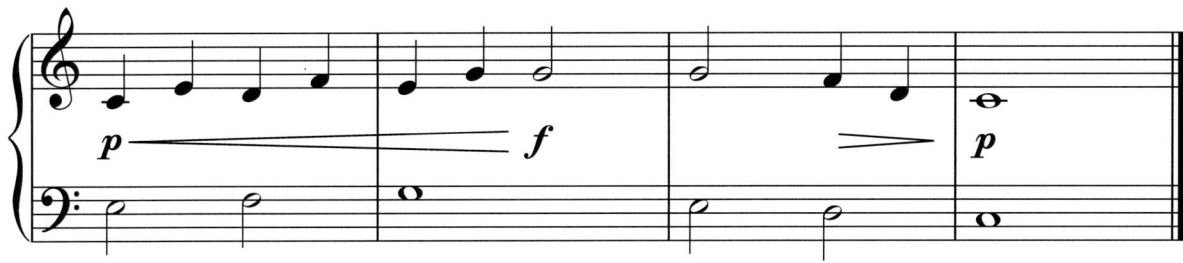

Highway

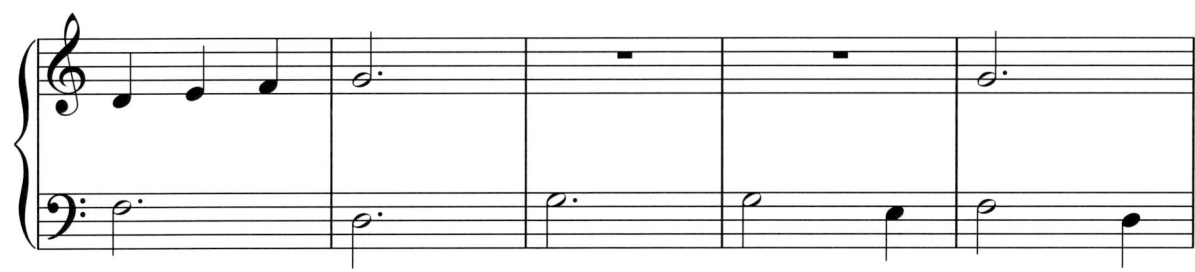
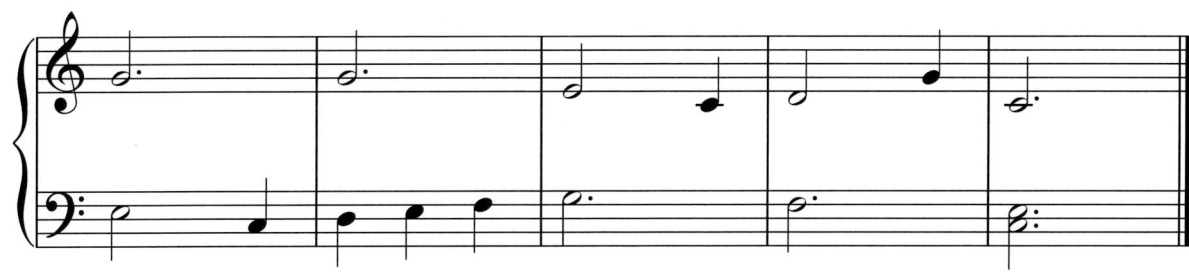

The Banks of the Ohio

Trad. arr. Alan Haughton

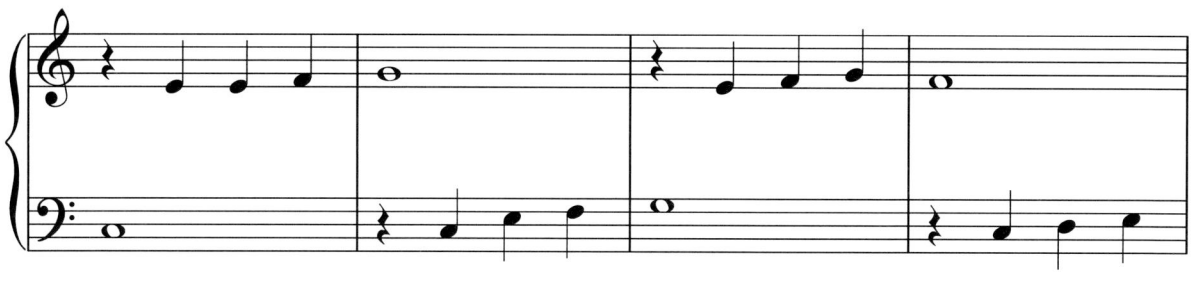

Ode to Joy

Ludwig van Beethoven arr. Alan Haughton

Moderately

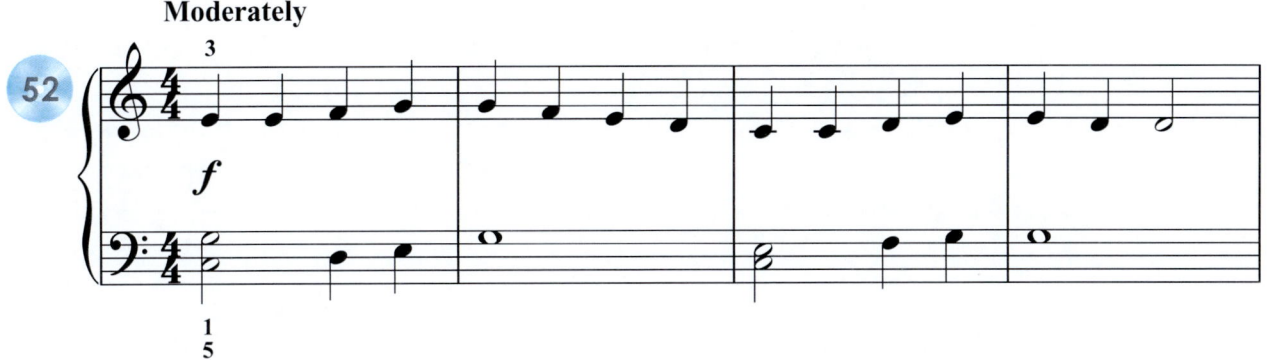
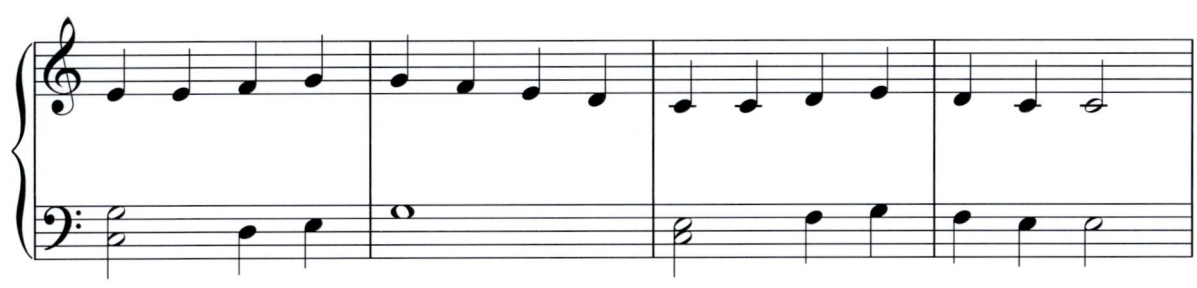

Sight-reading

> **Top Tip**
>
> Before playing, check the time signature and tap the rhythm. Look for 2nds and 3rds and check for patterns repeating. Make sure you know which fingers to use.

> **Top Tip**
>
> REMEMBER:
> The rhythm is just as important as the right notes.

If you are able to play through a piece accurately with the correct rhythm, pulse, notes and dynamics, then you are a good sight-reader.

Bouncing Bean

You may want to try this piece hands separately first.

Razzle Dazzle

Legato and Staccato

Know This

legato means to play the notes smoothly and connected.

staccato means to play each note short and detached.

You should play notes legato unless you see a dot over or under the note, which means you play that note staccato.

Try this short study.

Step on It

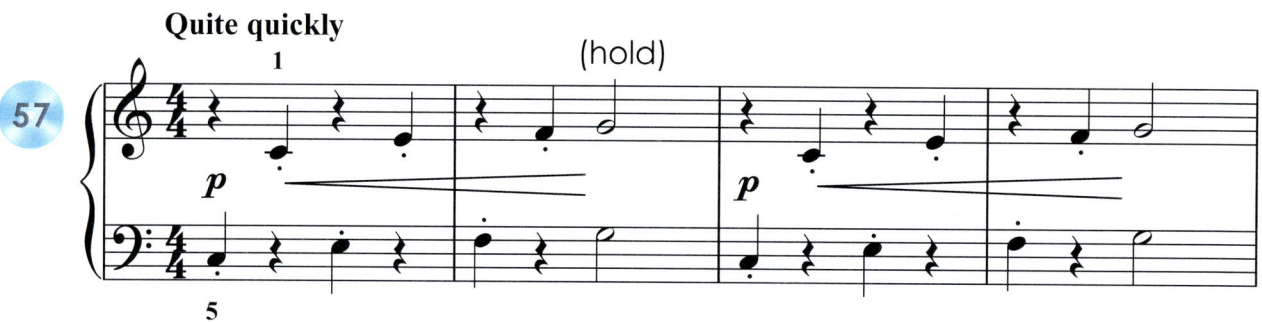

Rhythm Workout

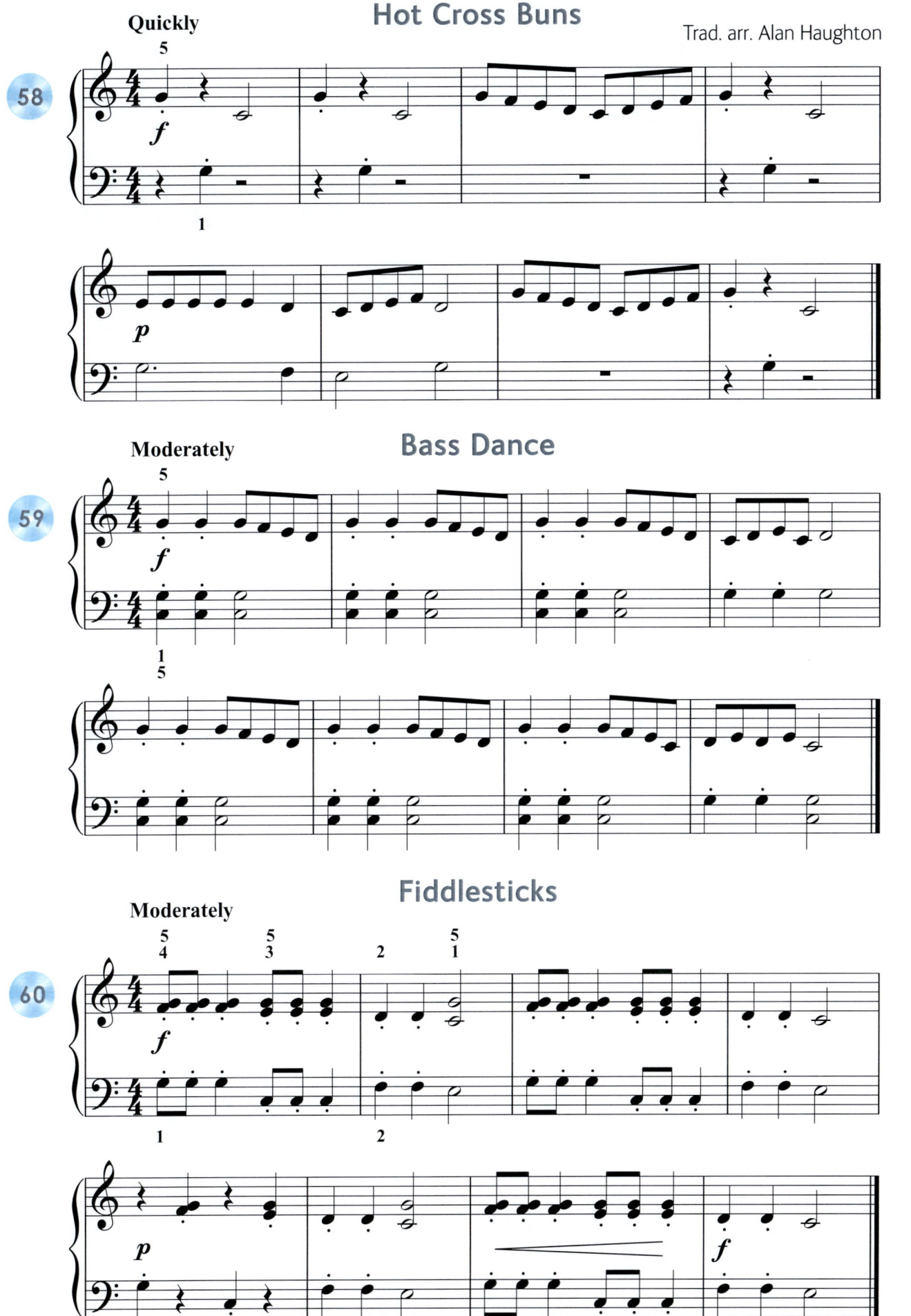

Super Trouper

Benny Andersson and
Björn Ulvaeus arr. Alan Haughton

French Folk Song

Trad. arr. Alan Haughton

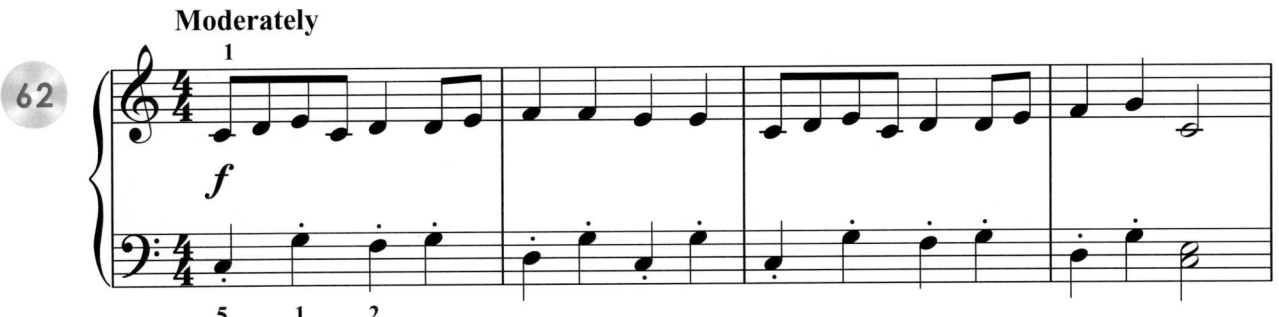

All of a Quaver

Know This

This is a quaver rest. 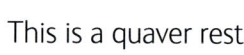 These are single quavers.

Quavers can also appear singly with a rest to make up the value of a crotchet beat.

Rhythm Workout 4

63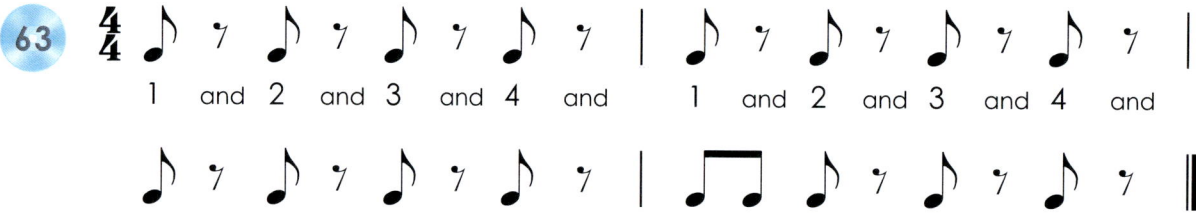

64

65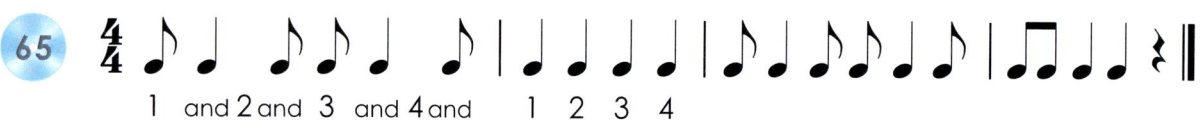

66

67

Hop, Skip and Jump

68

Pineapple

1, 2, 3, Go!

Quiz Time

How many beats?   What is the note's name?

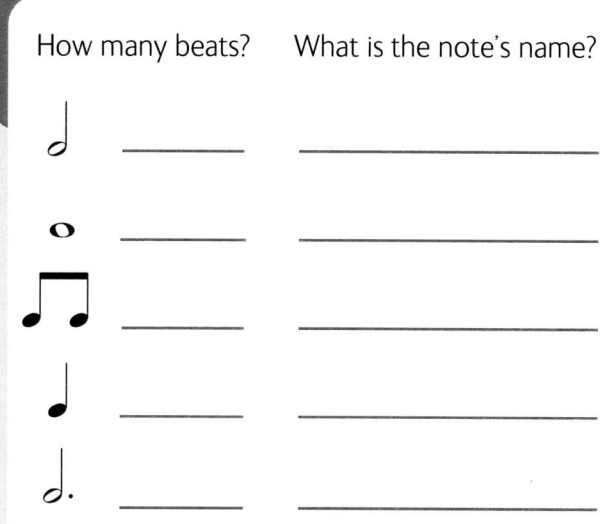

What do these letters mean?

p _____

mp _____

f _____

mf _____

What do these words mean?

legato _____

staccato _____

What do these signs mean?

_____

_____

Can you name these notes?

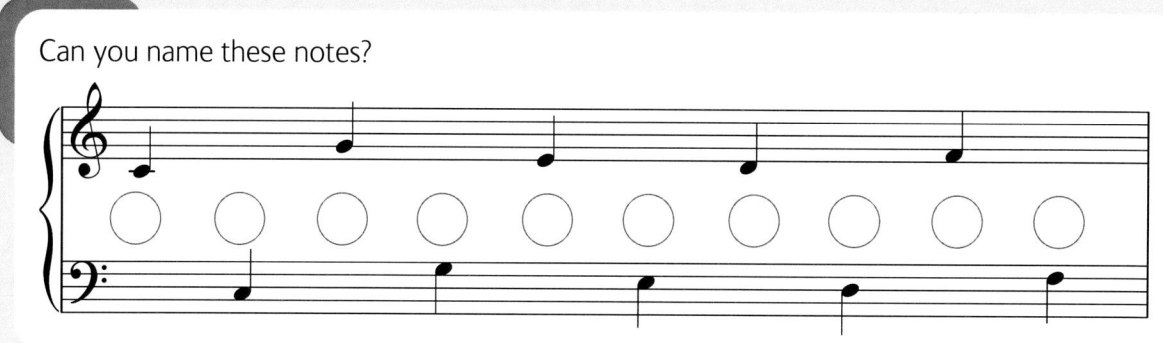

Write the time signature at the beginning of this music.

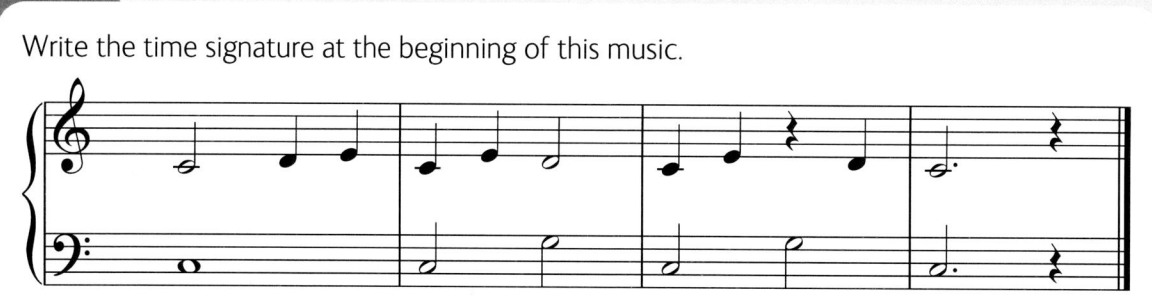

Concert Pieces

The Rock

Moderately

71

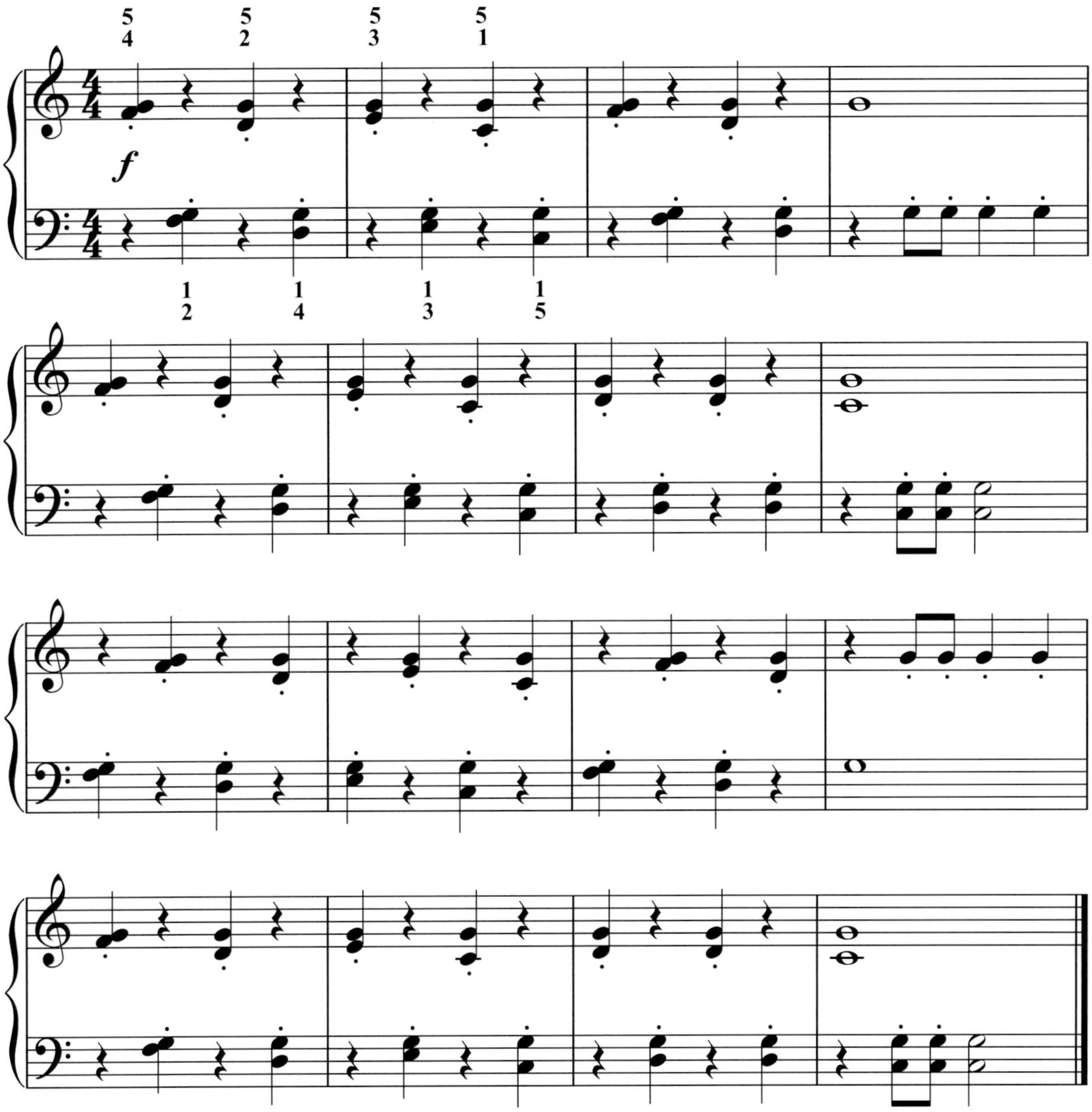

The Spiral Staircase

Quite slowly

72

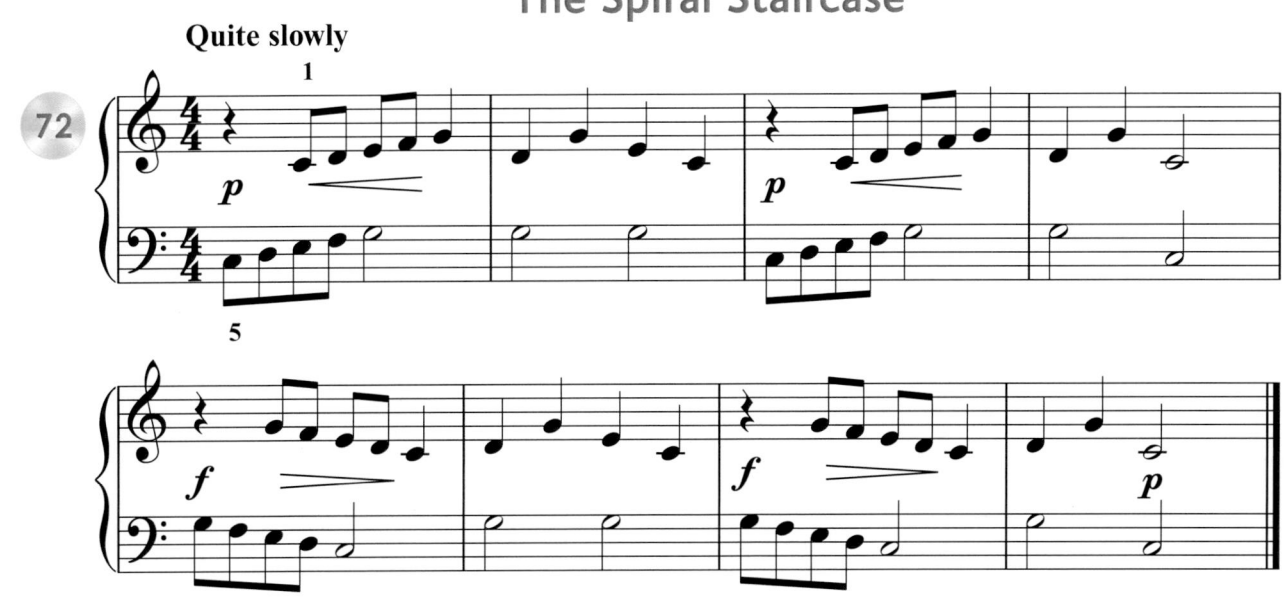

Gopak

Pick up Sticks

After the Storm

Trad. arr. Alan Haughton

Cockles and Mussels

Trad. arr. Alan Haughton

Shepherd's Hey

Trad. arr. Alan Haughton

This is A

Note

A comes after G!

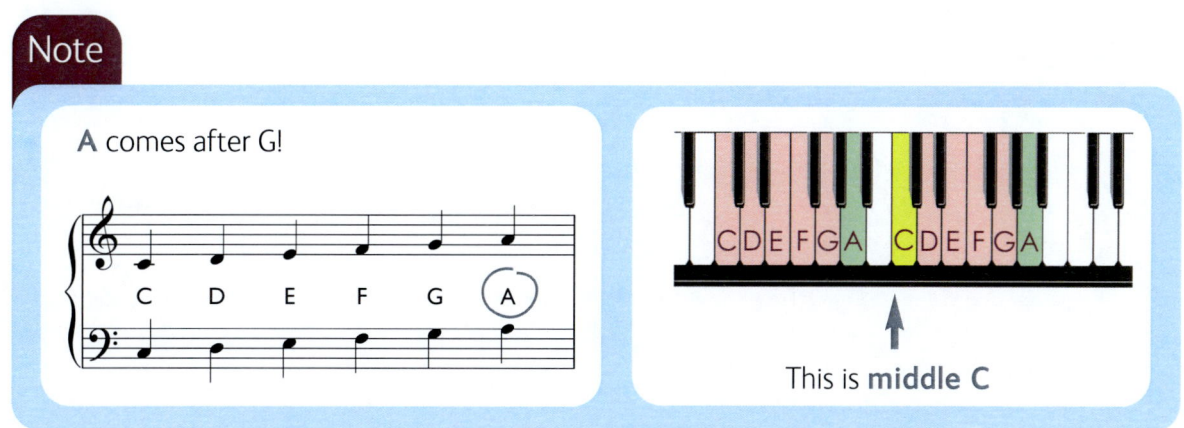

This is **middle C**

Top Tip

This is a new hand position with right-hand thumb on **D**.

Roxy's Waltz

Make sure you use your 3rd finger here!

2/4 Time

Know This

2/4 This time signature tells us there are two crotchet beats in a bar.

D.C. (Da Capo) means go back to the beginning. **al Fine** means play through to the end (where **Fine** is written). Fine means '**end here**'.

Tap these rhythms

Rhythm Workout 5

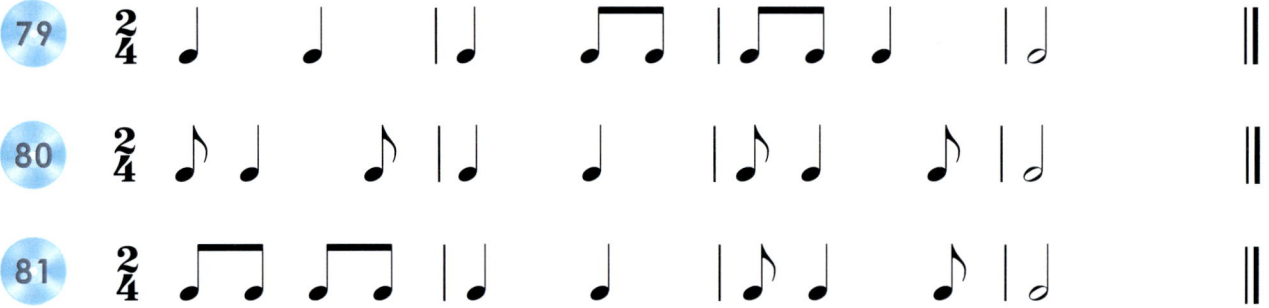

Jog It!

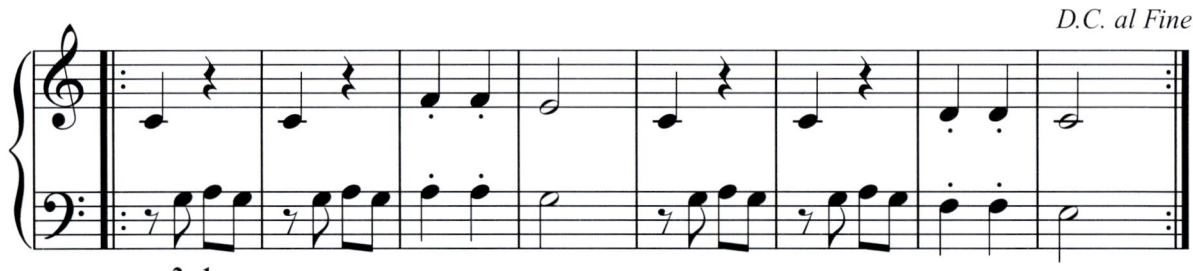

D.C. al Fine

Patterns

Can you see any patterns in these two pieces?
The right hand only uses fingers 1, 2 and 3.

1, 2, 3

Slalom

Right-hand B and C

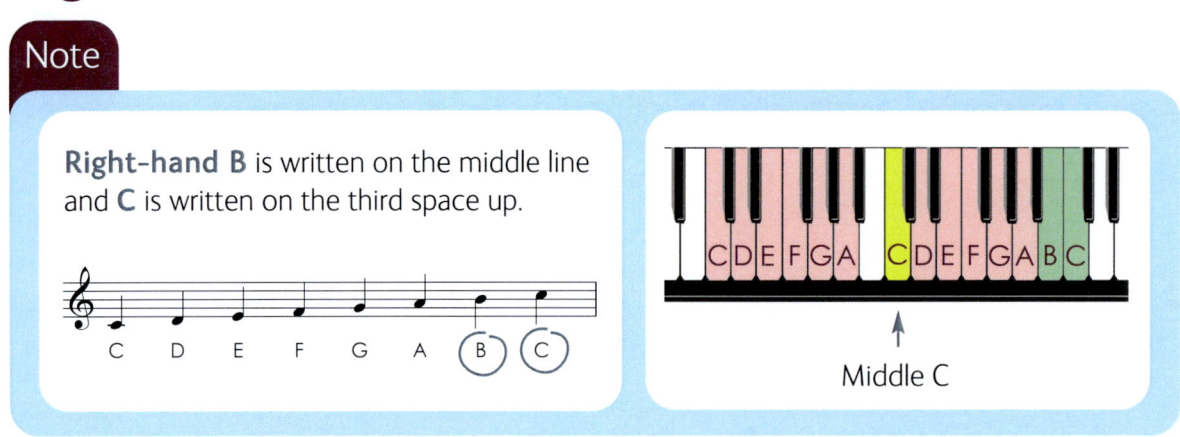

Note

Right-hand B is written on the middle line and **C** is written on the third space up.

There are two right-hand positions in the next piece – 3rd finger on B and 3rd finger on E. Change the position where you see ✱

Walk Tall

Lively

Know This

Italian words are often used to tell you how to play a piece of music. Tempo is an Italian word meaning speed. The tempo of a piece is given at the beginning.

Five popular tempo words are:
Adagio slowly
Andante at a walking pace
Moderato at a moderate speed
Allegretto quite quickly
Allegro quickly

There are two right-hand positions in 'High Street Rag' – 2nd finger on G and 3rd finger on E. ✻ shows you where.

High Street Rag

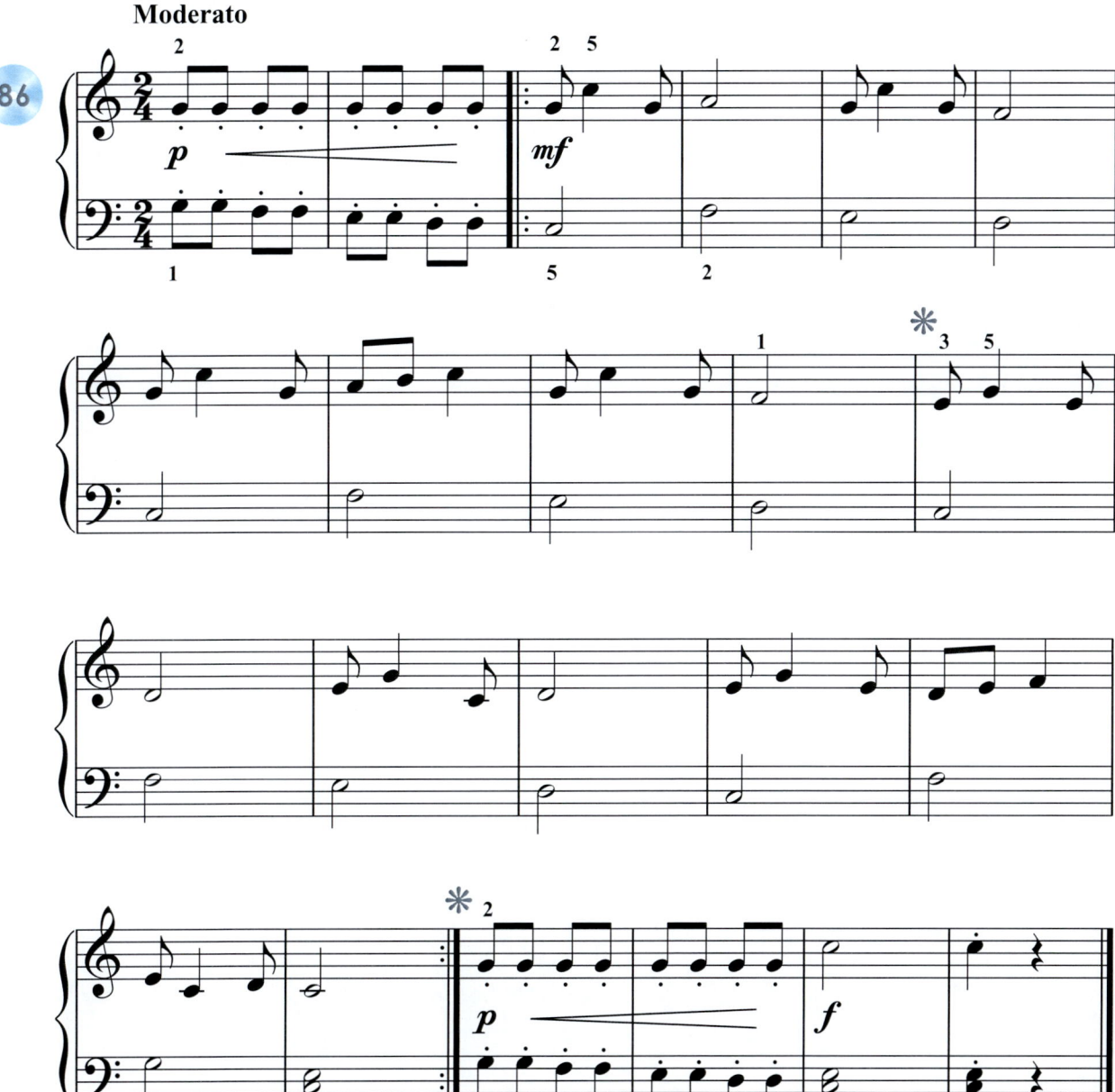

The Dotted Crotchet

Know This

You already know that a dot after a note makes it half as long again. A dot after a crotchet makes it worth a crotchet plus a quaver. (♩ + ♪) It is often followed by another quaver to make up two beats.

Rhythm Workout 6

Tap these rhythms.

87

88

89

Donkey Riding

Allegretto

Trad arr. Alan Haughton

90

Left-hand B and C

Note

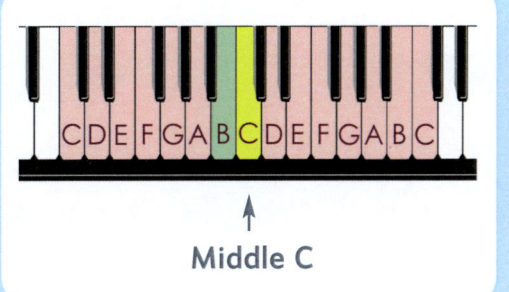

Middle C

B is written above the top line and **middle C** is written on its own line – called the leger line – as in the right hand, but it is written close to the bass clef stave and the tail goes down.

Snail

Adagio

Cycling

Allegretto

C Major Scale

There are seven different notes in a major scale.
The **C major scale** is the only scale which uses just white notes

> **Top Tip**
>
> Always use the correct fingering for scales.

Tuck your thumb under the 2nd and 3rd fingers to reach the F

Move your 3rd finger over your thumb

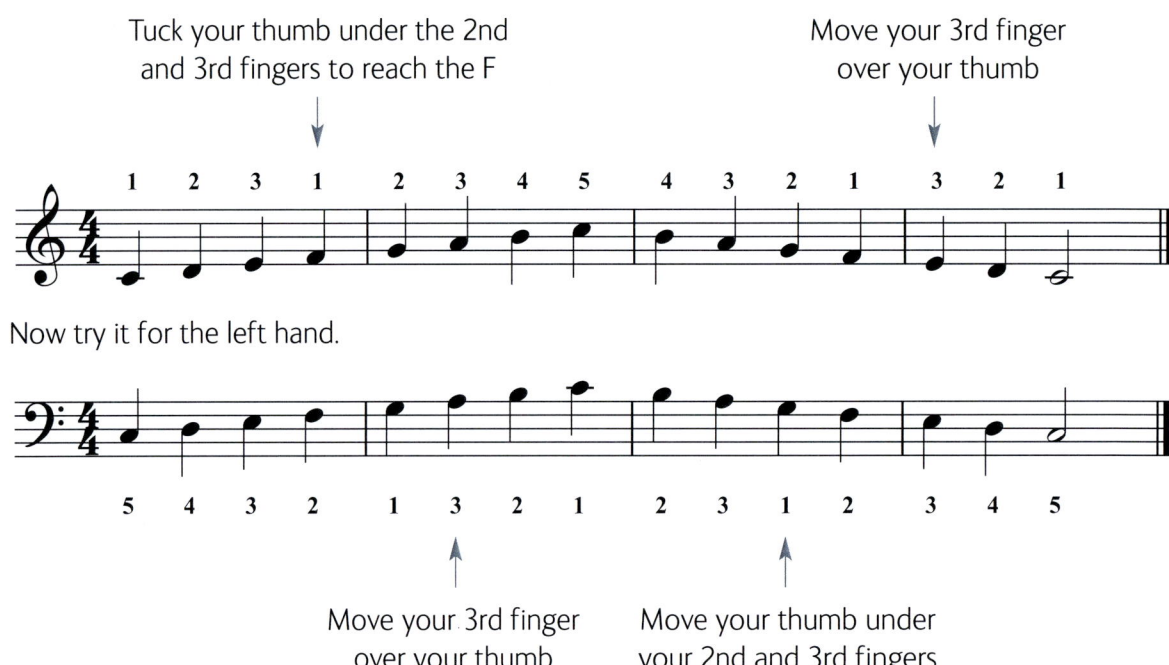

Now try it for the left hand.

Move your 3rd finger over your thumb

Move your thumb under your 2nd and 3rd fingers

Now play both hands together like this – it's called contrary motion.

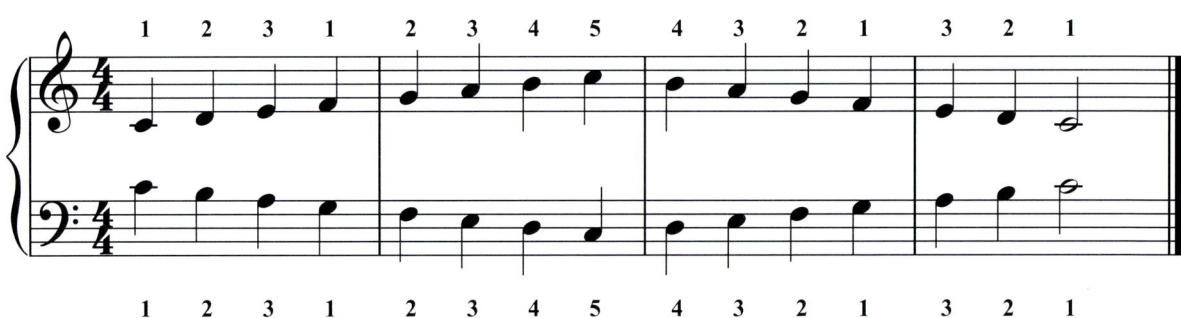

> **Know This**
>
> From one note to the same note 8 notes higher or lower is called an octave.

58

At the Gym

> **Scale Workouts**
> Use the given fingering to practise thumb under and 3rd finger over.

Thumb Workout

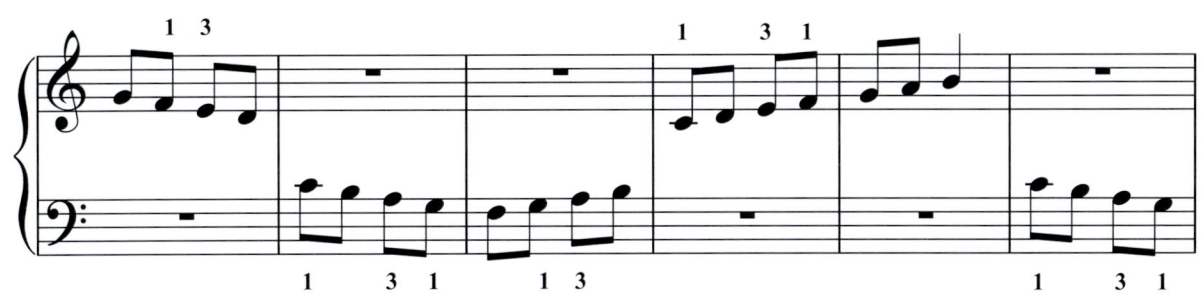

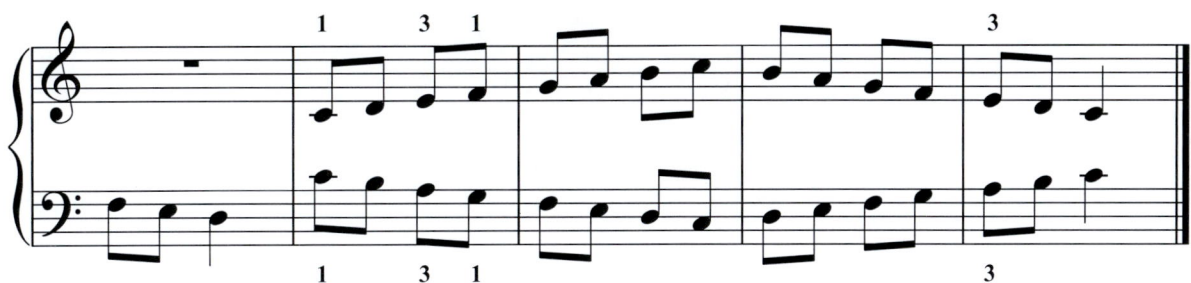

On the Scales

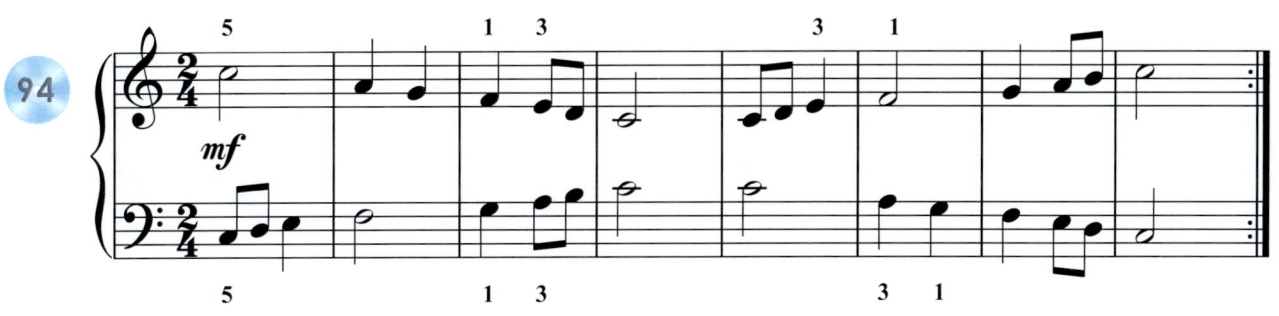

Scale Patterns

Try these tunes – they use scale patterns.

Jump to It

95

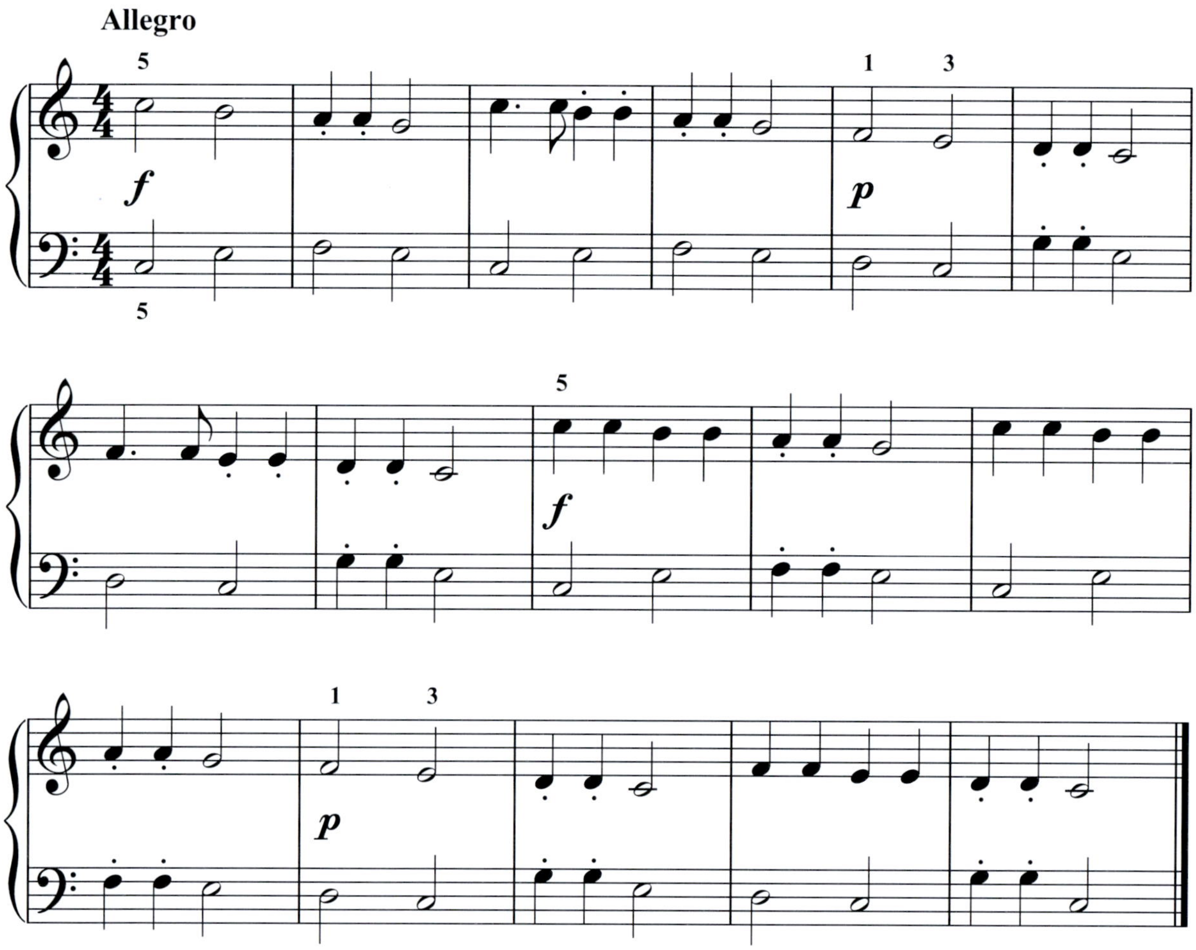

Butterfingers

96

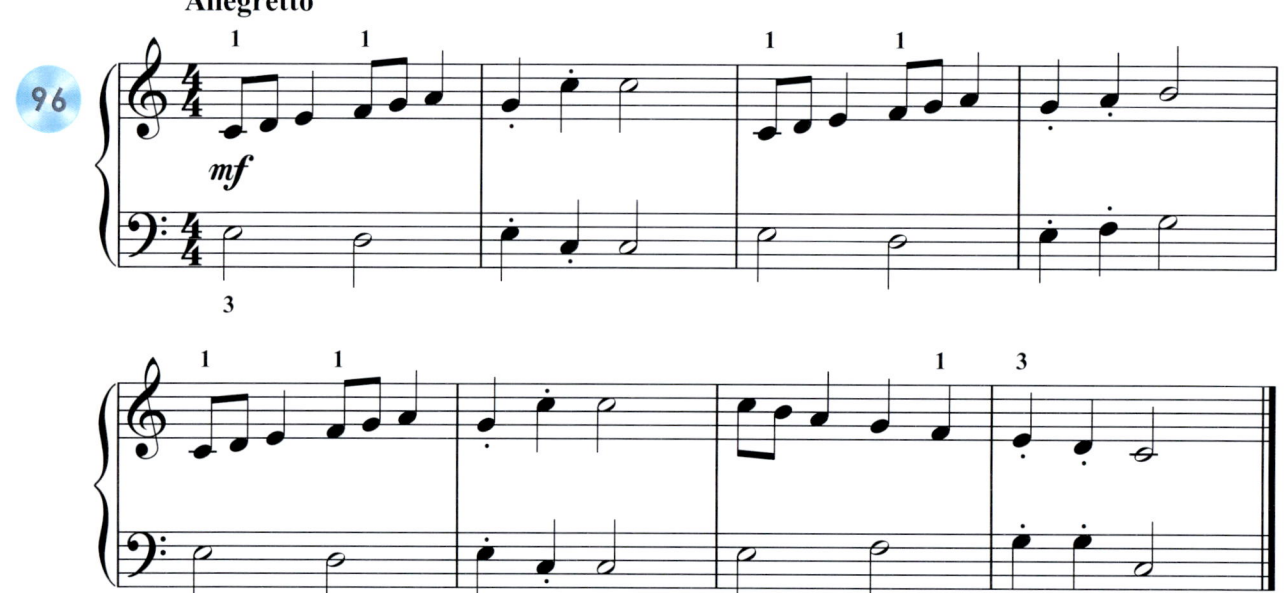

Quiz Time

Can you name these notes?

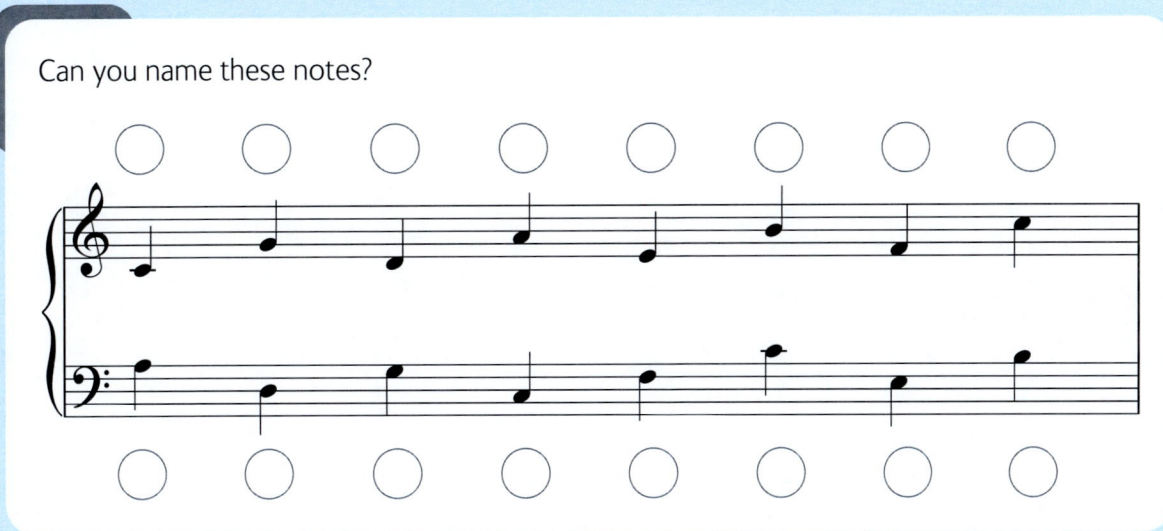

What do these mean?

D.C. al Fine _____

2/4 _____

3/4 _____

4/4 _____

How good is your Italian?
What do these words mean?

Tempo

_____

Allegro

_____

Allegretto

_____

Adagio

_____

Andante

_____

Moderato

_____

61

Concert Pieces

Popeye the Sailor Man

Sammy Lerner arr. Alan Haughton

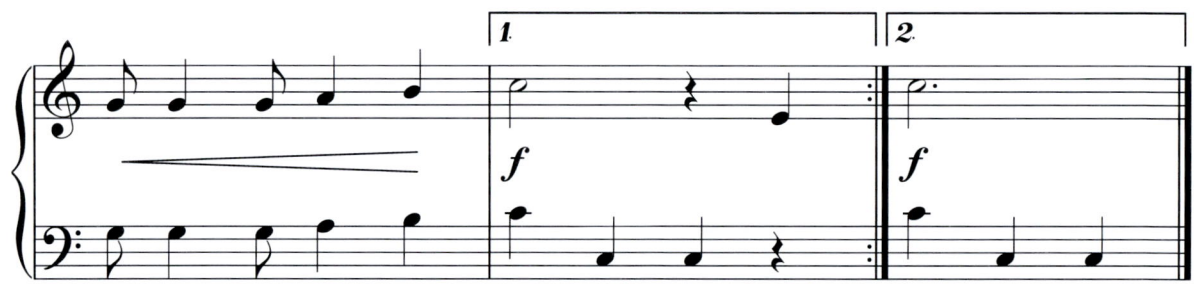

Papillon
(Butterfly)

Jingle Bells

James Pierpoint arr. Alan Haughton